# The Edu

## A Behind-The-Scenes Tale of Multimedia Intrigue

by Christopher Andrews

Wilton, CT
1993

ISBN 0-910965-10-2

Dedicated to
Emmie D. Mygatt.

# Table of Contents

# List of Plates

# Preface

I publish CD-ROMs and have a lot of fun doing it. This book contains stories about my adventures in the jungles of CD-ROM. Some stories are pleasant and lighthearted, and others are war stories I'd really like to forget. They are all the real stuff that CD-ROM is made of, though, with nothing held back.

The beauty and the challenge of CD-ROM is its versatility and its wide range of uses. As a result, I've always thought CD-ROM was a misunderstood technology. Some people think it's only good for data. Others think it's for pictures and sound. Some say it's the biggest success ever, while others say it's never going to make it. I wrote this book to show a complete picture of CD-ROM—from all sides.

I didn't invent CD-ROM, nor do I claim to be the ultimate CD-ROM historian, but my career has closely paralleled the development of CD-ROM. I have been involved in many ground-breaking projects—starting in libraries, moving to corporations, and then into multimedia. I've tried to show in this book the thread that holds together all these vastly different uses of CD-ROM. It is that thread that is the essence of CD-ROM.

Each of the stories in this book describes something that happened to me in my nearly decade-long love affair with CD-ROM. Though the stories are anecdotal in nature, beneath are answers to many fundamental questions about CD-ROM. In the back of the book is a glossary you might find fun to browse even if you don't have a specific word to look up.

If you're a living, breathing person then you either have a CD-ROM drive, have used one at the office or library, have read about CD-ROMs—or maybe you're even one of those people who talks about CD-ROM like an expert at cocktail parties. Whatever your level of involvement with CD-ROM, I hope you find this book enjoyable and informative. I hope it inspires you to dig deeper into an up-and-coming technology and industry.

Christopher Andrews
March 1993

# The Education Of A CD-ROM Publisher

## A Behind-The-Scenes Tale of Multimedia Intrigue

# one

## An Optical Disc? What's That?
## 1984

MY HEAD JERKED BACK, AND I FELT THE VIBRATION OF THE CHAIR tilting. Out of the corner of my eye, I could see a pair of forearms.

"Open wider," she said, looking through her jeweler's eyeglass into my mouth.

I felt the sharp pain of the metal pick bearing down on my gums. Anxiety heightened the pain, so I resorted to deep breathing to calm my nerves. "Breathe, breathe, breathe," I said to myself. It seemed to take hours, but when I leaned forward and looked at the clock, it had only been five minutes.

"I'll meet you in my office," she said, looking over her shoulder as she left the room. "I think we're all done."

I wandered back to her office and Terri Thor-Neumeyer, my new dentist, began describing proper flossing techniques. If I did it right once a day, she said, I wouldn't get gum disease. I was trying to read between the lines, wondering if she was telling me that I had gum problems, or were these just preventive measures? Since I didn't know her very well, I didn't know how seriously to take her advice. I decided that at least I wasn't in any immediate danger.

"What do you do for a living?" she asked. "Is it high stress?"

"It's pretty tense, but not too bad," I responded. "I'm in the information business."

"Oh, really, my husband is in the optical business. You should talk with him."

I couldn't figure out why I should get to know someone in the optical business, but I asked anyway.

"What does he make?" I said, imagining eyeglasses or lasers.

"He really doesn't make anything. He develops optical discs."

Bingo! "Optical discs" was the connection she was making. I was in the information business and her husband developed optical discs. "Optical disc" was one of the half-dozen terms people used to describe discs that are read by lasers. It was an umbrella for laserdiscs and compact discs, and usually implied using them in some computerized fashion, to store information. CD-ROM was the term being used for storing information specifically on a CD (compact disc).

I left and was intrigued about meeting someone else interested in optical discs. As I explained to her, I was in the online business, but had been researching optical discs ever since a spontaneous discussion at I.P. Sharp where I worked. I had been sitting around the office when the topic came up.

"That's unbelievable. Six hundred megs!" all the Sharpies were agreeing and saying in many different ways, including an occasional "No-o-o way." "Can you imagine what you could do with that much storage space?"

It *was* unbelievable what you could do with "600 megs." The computer industry, had a consistent pattern of making up cryptic, unapproachable words and acronyms, and "megs" or "megabytes" was no exception. What all this meant, though, is that on one of these optical discs you could fit 600 of these things—these megs, or "MB," which is the proper acronym.

When we added up 600MB, we found that all the I.P. Sharp databases could fit on just a few of these discs. And that information was now stored on an IBM 3081 computer, the largest and most expensive computer in the IBM line, sitting in an ultra-clean room on the 19th floor of the Sharp headquarters in Toronto. This room was impressive. It was the nerve center for the transmission around the world of massive amounts of information, 24 hours a day. It was the world's largest private network of information. It had local computers in many major cities around the world, including Moscow (but, of course, you wouldn't find the Moscow node on any of the promotional maps distributed in the U.S.). People from about every corner of the world could dial a local phone number and instantly connect to this 19th floor computer spectacle.

I.P. Sharp made $50 million per year in sales from this setup. Major companies would use this computer as their powerhouse companion, giving them instant access to huge amounts of data. Some customers used the computer with their own data, doing everything from international financial reporting to electronic mail communication. Other customers just used the I.P. Sharp databases. These databases, with information on everything from load statistics in the aviation industry to Australian economic data, were considered the world's largest collection of electronic numeric information in the world—millions of numbers.

And none of these databases were over 600MB. Any of them—or several—could fit on one optical disc!

That meant that the whole room on the 19th floor could be reduced to a bunch of optical discs that could be sent through the

Courtesy Optical Media International

*Allen Adkins, president of Optical Media International, had a vision for a CD-ROM publishing or premastering system. Here he stands in front of the first system that was built.*

mail. A customer could then just put it into a drive attached to a computer on their desk just like you might attach anything to a computer—or for that matter, just like plugging a tape deck or CD player into a stereo receiver. After all, tape decks, turntables, CD players, and optical discs all do the same thing: they send information—music or data or pictures—through a central controlling device and out some sort of output device. In the case of the stereo, the music always comes out the speakers. With the optical disc, being controlled by the computer, the information might come out on the computer screen or a printer or both.

Several weeks later, I called my dentist's husband. He gave me directions to his office in Mountain View, California, and before we got off the phone, he asked me what I did for work. I told him I was in the online business, and he asked why I'd be interested in optical discs. The connection—between the online business and optical discs—didn't occur to him as quickly as it did to his wife.

I arrived at his office late in the morning, and was greeted by Allen Adkins, an intense, distant man with large glasses. His office was located in an elementary school that had been converted into offices. The desks, tables, chairs, and general feel was still that of an elementary school. There were even some children's drawings still on the wall.

He sat me down next to a computer, which was on a table that looked like it had been the teacher's desk, and proceeded to type in several cryptic commands.

"There's more than a gigabyte right here," he said with all the pride of an inventor showing off his creation for the first time. "The real problem is

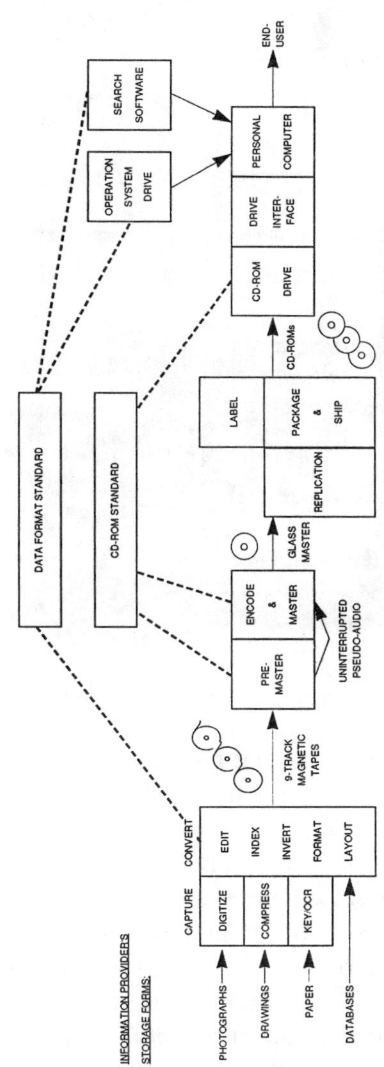


*The flowchart that described Adkins' system was a far cry from the online business.*

Photo courtesy of Optical Media International

*Adkins' vision eventually turned into a shippable product—the second one ever built is pictured here. With the premastering system, "in-house" CD-ROM publishing became possible.*

the premastering process," he continued. "There aren't any good tools, and that's why I'm building some. Here, look at this. I can put it all on a 3/4" Umatic tape and send it off to the factory to make a CD."

He showed me a chart that looked like a flow chart, but it had words I didn't understand—OCR, Premaster, Encode, Uninterrupted Pseudo-audio, Replication. These were strange words coming from the world of information, where "update," "numeric," and "text" were common terms. He then took the chart back as though he regretted ever showing it to me.

As I looked around his desk, I noticed not only the quantity of equipment, but the diversity and size. He truly was part inventor, mixed with some of the absent-minded professor, and a little high-tech entrepreneur. As Adkins described everything he did, he lost me less than half-way through. It wasn't that I didn't understand it, it was that my mind started to wander. I started thinking about the optical disc skeptics, and the fact that maybe they were right. After all, in the online business all I had to do was carry around a little portable terminal for dialing into Toronto. The optical business was starting to look very complex, almost like a factory on a desk. I felt dizzy, and realized that he and I weren't really speaking the same language. Either he had something up his sleeve he didn't want to tell me, or he just couldn't explain what he was doing. Or maybe I was just dumb.

My confusion about him, he also shared about me. As I told him more about the online business, and why I was excited about optical discs, he kept wondering why I had decided to call him. After an hour, I left more confused than ever. To my surprise, he gave me his flow chart.

I drove home thinking that some strange force was drawing me to this new technology. At the root of it was the conviction that information, like food and housing, should be easily available. With online systems costing several hundred dollars an hour, the little guy usually couldn't afford to use them. And, since they cost so much, the user had to be quick and efficient. This made sense for current information, but what about the mass of historical information that people should take their time searching through more serendipitously? The beauty of a book is the ability to go here and there, getting ideas from the book, and letting your imagination go. With the clock ticking, that rarely happens.

I spent much of the next several months on a search for information about optical discs. Surprisingly, I found nothing that remotely seemed to put it in language I could understand. All the magazines, especially electronics and engineering publications, seemed to be speaking Allen Adkins' language. Some magazines at the local Tower Records did, though, have great articles about the emergence of one type of optical disc, the compact disc. Music industry magazines were at odds over whether the CD was really going to meet the expectations that the original developers predicted.

Then it hit me. Allen Adkins builds printing presses and I write books. I thought about that over and over. It was an idea I could understand, and it made sense to steal a model from another industry. Allen was building a printing press so that people like me could make optical discs with information on them. He didn't care much about what went on those discs, and that's *all* I cared about.

I discussed the optical disc concept with many people at I.P. Sharp, trying through our electronic mail system to see if anyone else was doing something with this. I heard many good reasons why it wouldn't work. They ranged from the inability to update the discs frequently to the fact that someone could steal an entire library. Joey Tuttle, the vice president of technology and head of the Sharp PARC (Palo Alto Research Center) office, offered to steer me through the Sharp maze of people and personalities, as well as technologies. He wasn't too hopeful, however, about getting Sharp to back a CD-ROM project.

"Sharp is a specialized company of unique people, and what really ties us together is APL and a sophisticated network. The data, whether it is databases or stock market information or financial reports, is just that to us. It's just data. We don't collect the data, we just distribute it over a network, and provide software for using it."

Joey was well-liked at Sharp for his understated approach, and would frequently surprise top-level technical people with his seemingly easy grasp of complicated concepts. APL for him, and most people at Sharp, was a part of their life. They were known as APL'ers.

APL was a computer language designed to solve problems that other typical languages couldn't even touch. Stories of doing something in a week in APL that took a year in another computer language were common, and part of the lore of APL. The man who invented APL, Ken Iverson, worked at Sharp. APL was as much a religion as a programming language. It was made up entirely of Greek letters, and was highly visual, allowing you to solve problems at a high level. Though I didn't understand APL at the level of most people at Sharp, I, too, began to look at data visually rather than literally, which made it much easier to move across different types of data and information.

Rob Meyer, who worked in the database group for Sharp, thought the underlying reason why the Sharp databases would never make it on CD-ROM was frequency. He pointed out that many Sharp databases were updated daily. At the other end of the spectrum, though, were a number of annual databases. The line, between online and CD-ROM data, seemed to be working itself out as monthly. If the information was updated monthly or less frequently, it looked like a candidate for CD-ROM. Any more frequently, and online was best-suited.

It was an odd set of circumstances—realizing what Sharp could fit on optical discs, seeing the contraption in Allen Adkins' classroom, and reading everything from music to electronics magazines to discover this void that no one knew much about. What I found was a lot of loose ideas that were related, but no one knew just how. Eventually, those ideas started to form something identifiable and move on their own—something like a migration of birds flying south for the winter. You can't help but marvel at how these birds, so fragile, can overcome the elements and arrive safely. A bigger miracle is their ability to stick together like glue through their journey. Finally, they arrive at a nice warm spot to spend the winter days.

These fragile ideas about optical discs were flying around and were only there if you looked for them. If any of the people involved had realized how fragile those ideas were, and how difficult the trip, they never would have made the journey.

And that means they never would have arrived at CD-ROM.

# two

# InfoTrac: The First Product
## 1985

After five years at I.P. Sharp, I was ready for a move, and when I was offered a job at Information Access Company, it seemed like the perfect fit. IAC was an "information provider," whereas I.P. Sharp had been an information distributor. That meant, in my business, that I was getting closer to the raw information—closer to the source. I wanted to have more control over what information went on a network, instead of where the network sold the information. Plus IAC was involved in some projects that seemed closer than anyone else to putting the optical disc concept into action.

I had never had a job where I had to be at work at 8:00 in the morning. In fact, I was completely untrained in the proper behavior of a regular working situation, since work life at Sharp had always been somewhat of a social experiment. At

Sharp, everyone was equal, there was little formal attire, no real working hours, few planned meetings, and you only stayed if you fit in. If you did, you worked hard because you liked it. The company appealed to people who like a lot of privacy, because all the business of the company was done over the electronic mail network.

At Information Access Company, I not only got to work at 8:00 a.m., I usually had memos on my desk, needing my attention. It became apparent that there was a direct relationship between starting work at 8:00, replying to memos, and drinking coffee. I started to drink coffee. I also shared a small windowless office with someone, which was quite a contrast to my large private office with windows at Sharp. And moving from the cafe atmosphere of Palo Alto's California Avenue district to an office building off Highway 280 in Belmont, had me leaving home at an unbelievable 7:00 a.m.

A little bit by accident and a little by design, I found myself working for a company that was considered the pioneer in putting information on an optical disc. In this case, it wasn't CD-ROM, but a "12-inch optical disc." At this point, there was still much debate about which mass storage device would prevail as the leader in information distribution. InfoTrac, as the product was named, indexed and abstracted hundreds of thousands of magazine articles, and was sold to libraries.

I was amazed to see stacks and stacks of papers, magazines, journals and tabloids at IAC. Then I realized that collecting information, or being an information provider, was a dirty business—rubber gloves were common to protect hands from print ink. When you distribute information, you never see the raw materials; you only get a nice, clean floppy disk, or better yet, you only "touch" the information over a long-distance computer network. The arena at IAC was quite different. I got used

Courtesy Information Access Company

*Library patrons using one of the original InfoTrac systems. InfoTrac was developed in 1985, and provided local access, on an optical disc, to information that had previously only been available through an online service. Sign in middle of table says "Searches millions of articles in 10 seconds."*

to people introducing themselves by saying "I'm an indexer," or "I edit the abstracts."

Indexing is the backbone of information collection, and involves siphoning key characteristics of an article from a magazine or newspaper. For example, an index might contain the date of the article, name of the author, length of the article, and the all-important Subject Headings. The Subject Headings are usually words that describe that subject an article is about. If there was an article about the 1992 Presidential election, it might be indexed under the Subject Headings "Politics," "1992 Presidential Race," and "Campaigns."

Abstracting takes the process one step further and produces a brief or summary of the article, making sure to stay within guidelines to not infringe on the copyright of whomever owns the original article. Abstracts are usually anywhere from several lines to a paragraph in length. Indexing and abstracting are both about speed and conciseness. The indexers log the number of articles they index in a given period of time. I was shocked to learn that an article from a magazine could be indexed in five to ten minutes, and more shocked to learn that this was what was expected by the management at IAC. Though there was nothing wrong with working at that speed, what I had thought was intellectual work now seemed like an assembly line.

I was interested in optical discs, but I was the marketing manager for the Online Division. Within IAC, there was a fight for control of InfoTrac, and the other division, which produced and sold the microfiche systems to libraries, won. That meant that I could watch and feel InfoTrac, and use it as much as I wanted, but I had no say about the features. It was an interesting situation because it was the online people who knew about "searching," but the microfiche people who knew about hardware, installation, and direct sales. Therefore, the microfiche people were much more qualified to get InfoTrac into libraries, but we knew more about what to do with it once it was there. At trade shows, I found myself spending more time showing InfoTrac than I expected, and I marveled at how librarians couldn't seem to get enough of it.

My main job was to manage a relationship with Dialog, the world's largest seller of online information. Dialog had been started by Dr. Roger Summit, who designed an online system to solve a problem at Lockheed, the original owner of Dialog. Dialog and IAC had a tough and sometimes bitter relationship.

IAC really started as a company on the heels of Dialog. Dialog was the only source of revenue for IAC's online division because it was an exclusive relationship. IAC could not sell its information elsewhere, even though two other companies, BRS and Mead Data Central (known for its LEXIS/NEXIS service) had approached it about selling information through their services, which were competitors of Dialog.

*Morry Goldstein, president of Information Access Company, and Dr. Roger Summit, founder of Dialog, pictured here with Jeff Pemberton, founder of Online Inc.*

The exclusive contract that IAC and Dialog signed five years earlier was coming up for renewal. IAC had grown up since then, and was ready to do business with its two other suitors. The presidents of Dialog and IAC were arguably the two most prominent and respected people in the information industry. Roger Summit was known for his thoughtful, prodding vision that helped develop the online information industry. Morry Goldstein was the charismatic personable leader of IAC, who was known as much for his image and confidence as for the substance of his leadership.

After many months of negotiating the finer points of a large exclusive contract, Dialog finally resigned itself to the fact that IAC was going to leave the nest. I personally disagreed with this change, primarily from a revenue point of view because Dialog was cutting the royalties in half in return for dropping the exclusivity. Since these databases were the most popular on the Dialog system, this meant an immediate windfall for Dialog, and a decrease in revenue by one-half for IAC. The idea, of course, was that this would be made up by putting the information on the other two online services. However, since all IAC's revenues were based on the amount of usage, it seemed unlikely that the other two services, which had a much lower presence in the library community, could make up the difference.

Since it was "necessary for the future of the company," though, I went along with this change. After all the positioning and innuendoes, we finally had the first meeting between Morry Goldstein and Roger Summit. It was to sign the contract and was in Summit's corner office in Palo Alto, looking out over Los Altos Hills. Blodwen Tarter, my boss at IAC, and Stan Skudneski, the person from Dialog with whom I had worked on the contract, were also there.

At another level, IAC was also a Dialog competitor, by offering its information on optical disc. InfoTrac gave IAC the ability to bypass Dialog completely and sell information directly to the customer. IAC also entertained the idea of licensing information from third parties for inclusion on InfoTrac, which was being marketed as a system that could handle multiple discs. Summit, in direct response to the threat of InfoTrac and the CD-ROM concept, issued several strong statements. In the December 1985 *CHRONOLOG* newsletter that went out to Dialog's customers he wrote:

*1986 will be the key year in which decisions will be made with regard to the CD...Users will be tempted by CD-based database products which will require that they acquire as yet unproven CD-ROM players and discs. Although there has been substantial experience with audio players, there is relatively little field experience with the personal computer-oriented CD-ROM drives and discs...Database producers are being invited to offer their databases under a variety of contractual arrangements, some of which may have unintended and undesirable effects...CD-ROM updates are expensive and time-consuming to produce and distribute...You can be sure that when Dialog offers a CD-ROM product it will have the same degree of quality and support we insist on for our other products and services.*

"Tempted," "unproven," "undesirable." The emotion behind the words was evident and the message was clear. Summit was telling the customers not to buy CD-ROM products. The database producers, with which Dialog had a virtual monopoly when it came to online distribution, were being advised not to deal with the likes of IAC. Wait for Dialog to figure out what to do, Summit appealed. Summit had another reason to worry about CD-ROM. Since most of Dialog's databases were updated monthly, unlike I.P. Sharp which sold information that was updated more frequently, Dialog databases were perfect candidates for CD-ROM. Furthermore, Dialog had not signed contracts with any of its database suppliers to give Dialog the right to make a CD-ROM.

The contract between IAC and Dialog was signed, and the relationship quickly changed. IAC went from "preferred nation status" to being just another database supplier on the Dialog network.

The same month Summit's *CHRONOLOG* article appeared, another publication was picking up the significance of what was happening. "Compact Disk Technology Is Finding New Niches in Computer Data Field," read a *Wall Street Journal* article. "The availability of useful business information might give compact disks a boost as successors to microfiche and supplements to on-line databases." The language was not much more positive than Summit's, saying that CD-ROM "might supplement" online databases.

It was not just the technology that was emerging, but the industry and infrastructure that would support the development and distribution of the products. Though no one knew yet if it was "CD ROM," "CD/ROM" or "CD-ROM," and "disk" or "disc," everyone wanted a piece of it. Holding one in my hand, it seemed to possess mystical powers. I realized that I wanted a piece of it—I just wasn't sure which piece.

# three

## Meganews in New Canaan
## 1986

IN A SMALL ROOM IN THE UNITED AIRLINES COURTESY LOUNGE IN the San Francisco airport, I sat across the table from Dan Jones. Dan was an energetic man, always well-dressed, and he was the president of a company named NewsBank. On a tip from an old friend, I had written NewsBank a letter looking for a job. And on this Sunday, Dan was offering me a job—Product Manager for CD-ROM.

Before that red-letter day, I had made countless phone calls—NewsBank was the only company I could find that was committed enough to CD-ROM to have a job that included "CD-ROM" in its title. Many companies were skeptical, and most just plain didn't understand what CD-ROM was, or like Dialog, had the attitude that the best offense is a good defense.

NewsBank was not a large company. It employed about 100 full-time people, and another 100 home-based indexers, who came to pick up newspapers, indexed them at home, and returned the results. NewsBank was founded by John Naisbitt, author of *Megatrends*, but Dan bought the company from Naisbitt and was now the sole owner. Immediately, I noticed the consistency between NewsBank's concentration on local and regional newspapers, and *Megatrends*' emphasis on regional trends and content analysis. In the introduction to *Megatrends*, Naisbitt says, "Our group collects information about what's going on locally across the country and then looks for patterns." NewsBank, with its daily indexing of 500 local and regional newspapers, was obviously one of the best sources for learning what's going on locally.

What made NewsBank really unique, though, was that it was located on Pine Street in New Canaan, Connecticut. It was about the only real business in New Canaan, except for the gift shops and grocery stores. What's more, it just so happened that I had gone to high school in New Canaan. I left the day I graduated, swearing I'd never return to this wealthy town that is always ranked near the top when it comes to per-capita income in the U.S. New Canaan was rich, no doubt about it—and, as a California liberal, I was a "stranger in a strange land."

As a sign of things to come, Dan offered me a job on Sunday, in California—and he wanted me to start two days later—in Connecticut. I, of course, couldn't say no, so I packed my bags on Monday, and was on a plane Tuesday. I flew back to NewsBank in New Canaan, Connecticut—the only company that would hire a full-time CD-ROM person, in the only town I swore I'd never return to.

NewsBank's business was collecting several hundred regional newspapers, and processing them through an intellectual refining

Photo courtesy of NewsBank, inc.

*The NewsBank Electronic Index changed NewsBank from a print and microfiche company to a technological leader. Notice the front panel that not only instructs the user, but protects the CD-ROM, which is behind the panel, from being removed.*

machine of people that sorted, organized, indexed, input, printed, and delivered the resulting information to libraries. The product was a printed index to the newspapers, arranged by subject, and organized by a code that enabled you to find the original article on microfiche, which NewsBank also sold. The information was powerful, allowing you to investigate any issue or trend and find the raw data: what people thought in specific areas of the country.

My job was to put the product on CD-ROM, so that instead of leafing through volumes of books to find articles about popular research topics such as crime or the environment, you'd select them on a computer screen, and print out what you wanted.

When it came time to test the NewsBank Electronic Index, I contacted my high school teacher and coach, Mr. Borgman. He was a well-liked teacher, still at New Canaan High School, and I decided it would be great to use his class to test the CD-ROM.

He agreed, and we lugged the computer and CD-ROM over to the high school. The most important testing device was a stop-watch. We figured that speed was the only reason people would pay several thousand dollars more for the CD-ROM instead of the printed product. We had to feel confident that the CD-ROM would beat the book. One student sat at the computer, and the other used the book. Each had a list of questions to answer.

After a day of testing, the first real "benefit" of the NewsBank Electronic Index was clear. Typically, students were answering questions in less than five minutes from the CD-ROM that could take up to a half-hour with the thick volumes of the printed index. A printout also saved the time of writing things down. Given the list price of over $5000 per year, we felt fortunate the tests had come up with some hard evidence to support the price.

I packed up the computer gear and stopped by Mr. Borgman's classroom, and we sat alone in the square room. As we talked, I was reminded of one of the main reasons I had left New Canaan. New Canaan usually had the best high school tennis team in the state, and Mr. Borgman was the coach.

I had moved to New Canaan from Palo Alto, California while I was in high school, and felt confident about playing tennis on the East Coast. Palo Alto was considered the mecca of the tennis boom in the United States during the height of tennis popularity in the '60s and early '70s. It had the top high school, top junior college, and top university in the country for tennis.

Though I didn't lose a match in the regular season that year, I did lose in the state tournament to the #2 player behind me at New Canaan High School, Harlan Stone. It was a controversial tournament and I wanted nothing more that to get back to California after it was over. A number of people suspected a rigged tournament, but I thought they didn't like me because I was from California.

Mr. Borgman and I laughed about it, recalling how red his face had become when he got angry. I got up to leave, anxious to report the results of the CD-ROM test to Dan Jones. Maybe New Canaan wasn't so bad after all, I thought. I told him I was flying the next week to the Midwest to install the first NewsBank CD-ROM, and how excited everyone at NewsBank was because it was the first monthly CD-ROM to be sold. It also looked like we were going to beat the ALA (American Library Association) deadline. We wanted a system installed before the ALA conference to strengthen our marketing position.

As I walked out, Mr. Borgman said, "Hey Chris." I turned and looked over my shoulder.

"Call me Dan," he said.

# four

## Shepard's Pie and Alphabet Soup
## 1986

THE "INFORMATION INDUSTRY" IS A LOOSELY-KNIT GROUP OF companies who are involved in producing, distributing and selling information. Traditionally, the companies include online services (selling information over a computer network), phone companies, and companies that publish information electronically. When CD-ROM arrived on the scene, it became part of the information industry. The Information Industry Association (IIA) in Washington, DC is a trade and lobbying organization for this group of companies.

The language of the information industry includes such terms as: 9600 baud, free-text searching, records, fields, fixed-field, hierarchical indexes, and that nerd of all technical terms—Boolean searching.

Explaining Boolean searching takes people back to their grade school days, trying to understand the significance of Venn diagrams. Remember all those circles, overlapping, creating new shapes, resembling an octahedron with curves—A plus B but not C near to D is enough to create anxiety in anyone. It must've been a Communist plot that Mr. Boole and Mr. Venn, who lived at about the same time in the 1800s, cooked up to confuse the cultural elite.

To make matters worse, Webster's Dictionary describes Boolean as:

*"A deductive logical system, usually applied to classes, in which, under the operations of intersection and symmetric differences, classes are treated as algebraic quantities."*

Huh?

Boolean searching is the hallmark of the online library community. Most librarians not only know what it is, they are experts at it. They can cruise into an online service at unimaginable speeds, and pull off information in seconds flat. If you looked at the trail they left behind on their computer, you'd see a line of cryptic characters, all designed to tell the computer "Find what I'm looking for, and find it fast, because I'm scared as hell of the $200 per hour I'm paying to do this."

It never really made sense, once CD-ROM became a viable alternative, to keep information on a million-dollar computer 3,000 miles away. Why use a complicated networking system to access the computer and find out, for example, where to locate articles written in 1989 about political action committees? The staff, equipment, cost, and complexity are overkill for this type of information. On the other hand, if you want to find out what happened in the stock market last week, using an online service is great. The line between remote (i.e., online) and local (i.e., CD-ROM) information access has become blurred, as computers get smaller and faster, and people learn how to make CD-ROMs accessible over a phone line or network.

One ongoing controversy in the CD-ROM community is whether or not Boolean searching is appropriate for the typical CD-ROM. CD-ROM does not usually have the same sense of urgency, and doesn't need software that is as precise or powerful. On a CD-ROM, it is typically more important for the learning curve to be short, which allows anyone to walk up and start using a product without any training.

Shepard Broadfoot was the vice president of sales at NewsBank for many years, and spoke with a smooth Southern accent. His job was to sell the NewsBank service to thousands of libraries. With the advent of our CD-ROM product, he had to manage a group of salespeople trying learn to sell CD-ROM instead of books and microfiche. It's not an easy transition, and it was obvious from the beginning that some salespeople saw it as the "wave of the future," while others thought it was a gimmick. Convincing the sales force was complicated by the librarian in March 1986 who objected to CD-ROM—and explained with confidence, "CD-ROM is nothing. I'm waiting for CD-I."

Shepard's job, on the other hand was to sell, and he was good at it. He'd squint, light up another cigarette with his elbow resting on his knee, and say, "Explain to me again why we don't have bouillon searching?" His personality was magnetic, and he was without a doubt the most popular guy on the trade show circuit.

"It's Boolean, Shepard," I'd say. "Boo-lee-in. It's not soup."

Whether he did it on purpose or not, I'll never know, but "bouillon" searching was how Shepard pronounced it, and that's how it became known at NewsBank. It seemed that once Shepard spoke the words, everyone felt comfortable saying it. "Bouillon," they'd say, with just a hint of rebellion.

I'd then explain to Shepard that Boolean searching meant that the user had to type in words to find things, and often that involved some skill. And, since NewsBank used a hierarchical index with main topics, subtopics, etc., Boolean searching didn't work well on it. Boolean searching worked best with a wealth of words that could be searched, compared, and presented to the user. A hierarchical index is intentionally concise and sparse. Usually, after I explained these esoteric concepts, he'd take a deep breath, and look at me as though he was sorry he ever asked the question.

Then I'd start to explain it in a more friendly fashion. For example, if you wanted to find information about old houses in Connecticut, I'd tell him, you might type in: *old and houses and connecticut.*

But what if you were really looking for "Bungalows built in New England before 1900?" Or just "Farmhouses?" Well then you might have to type in: *(old and houses and connecticut) or (bungalows and "new england" < 1900) or farmhouses.*

And what if it came back and said: *There are 5,592 matches to your request.*

Shepard would look at me with suspicion, and the hint of a grin, as though he was saying, "Boy, you are nuts." Shepard and I never really had a meeting of the minds, and I'm sure whatever I did only confirmed what he thought about people who work too closely with computers.

The picture of a typical person trying to find something using Boolean searching was generally not a pretty one. Most people consider Boolean searching a necessary evil. It's easy to see how a Boolean request can quickly grow in length and complexity, and still not bring an untrained person the answers he or she wants.

NewsBank's hierarchical searching scheme took advantage of a highly structured printed index, and gave users choices instead of asking them to type in words. Given the previous example, a user of the CD-ROM might be presented a list of major topics—subject headings. Looking at the choices, one might be "Homes and

Housing" and the user would say, "Aha," and select that topic. Another heading under the first one might be called "Antique," which would provoke another "Aha." This technique of browsing, going into and out of topics, usually prompted users to find what they wanted instead of presenting them with a blank screen.

Eventually the user would go work his way down the hierarchical menus, narrowing down his topic. The advantage is that this kind of searching tends to lead people, instead of offering the hit-and-miss approach of Boolean. Boolean, on the other hand, uses the power of the computer to find relationships between words instead of just the hierarchical index that was produced by a person and put into the computer.

Since the NewsBank product appeared, millions of dollars have been spent trying to improve on this aspect of CD-ROM, and improve information retrieval in general. Most projects try to improve two aspects: recall (finding as much correct information as possible) and precision (making that information precise, accurate, relevant). There have been some successes, but most are variations where the user types in a word or browses a list of pre-defined words.

Two effective ways to guide a user through this maze are by using a thesaurus in Boolean searching and cross-references in hierarchical searching. With the thesaurus, the computer will automatically search for synonyms of a word. For example, the user might type in "mansions" and the computer would also automatically search "houses," or vice versa. With cross-references, the user might see "mansions" on the list of words, and it would say "See Homes and Housing." It's the same general concept.

Another area of great promise for information retrieval is relevance ranking, intelligent searching, or, if you stretch it, artificial intelligence. Compton's NewMedia was one of the first CD-ROM producers to pioneer the concept of doing some thinking for the user, though that comes at a risk. Harold Kester, started a company named Del Mar Group that was acquired and became part of Compton's NewMedia. He designed Smartrieve, Compton's access software. His description of the strategy behind Smartrieve shows the complex issues involved in making computers search for words:

*Smartrieve is designed to maximize both recall and precision in information retrieval. This enables users to find as many possible relevant records, by typing in any combination of words they want, in any order. Because Smartrieve tends to find a maximum number of relevant records (based on the theory that it is better to find a large quantity of records, then see how relevant they are, rather than miss records which could be relevant), those records are then ranked according to how relevant they are to the search.*

*...The algorithm for retrieval is then "tweaked" to best represent the database, and a score of 99 is given as the highest. This high score would generally mean that all words were found in the record, and there was representation of the words in the heading level. If a record is listed, but has a relevance score of closer to 0, then that record would probably only remotely be related to the query, but we still find this useful to present to the user for their perusal.*

*Smartrieve is used mostly by people who are not information professionals, and therefore do not have experience searching large databases. This requires some innovative approaches to "hooking them in," so they can quickly have success and will want to continue. The ability of Smartrieve to present the user with a large list, which is sorted by relevance, is a bit riskier than the normal Boolean method based on fewer criteria, but the results are often worth it. Users find things, or come up with ideas, that they may not have through other means.*

At NewsBank, the software, information, CD-ROM publishing process, and hardware assembly were all homegrown. A programmer named Steve Hutton spent countless hours building software and a process to allow us to ship a new updated disc every month that could easily be used in a library. Since most libraries were putting CD-ROMs out for public use, near the card catalog, it had to be simple and easy, like an automated teller machine. This was not an easy task, since most people had never used a computer to look something up. However, an intriguing phenomenon appeared in the high schools and colleges using the NewsBank CD-ROM: group research. Students would sit around in a group and use the CD-ROM to look things up together, sometimes having quite a bit of fun in the process. To them it was a far cry from the thick reference books in the reference section—that contained the same information but in an old and boring format.

Computerized information retrieval is as much an art as a science. The prospect of developing a single software program that can search many kinds of information is bleak, because of the inherent differences in various kinds of information. Scientific, economic, or business databases may appear similar, but storing and retrieving the information from each may require very different tools.

There is one promising search method on the horizon, though, and it's called Bouillon Searching (or Shepard's Pie). What you do is squint your eyes at the computer, look at it as though you wish you had never entered your query, sigh, put your elbow on your knee, then just go home. Make some bouillon and forget it. Go from high-tech to high-touch. After all, there was a time when alphabet soup was all you needed for whatever ailed you. It might still work.

# five

## How to Kill a CD-ROM

## 1986

IT STARTED AS ONE OF THOSE THINGS THAT COULD BE JUST AN isolated incident or a full-blown catastrophe. We had shipped the latest NewsBank CD-ROM to about 50 libraries, when we received several seemingly unrelated calls from customers complaining that the disc didn't work.

"Is the disc in the drive?" the NewsBank customer support people were trained to ask.

"Yes," each caller would say.

"Is it in there with the NewsBank label pointing up?" was the next query.

"Yes," came back the reply.

The NewsBank customer support people had been trained in a hilarious morning session about how to handle the phone inquiries. They spent most of their training time with their backs to me, while I pretended to be a customer with questions. They'd have to ask me questions and lead me through solving the problems. The odd results often caused some good belly laughs—like the time they told me to do everything but turn the computer on. You can imagine their surprise when they turned around to find me giving commands just as they instructed—to a dead computer. Despite such stumbling blocks, I was surprised at how quickly this spirited group picked up the subtleties of supporting computers, which is quite a leap from answering questions about books.

After a dozen people called with these mysterious symptoms, it began to take on the air of an epidemic, and I knew it was different from anything we had seen. There had been much press coverage about the volatility of CD-ROM, and whether it was ready for wide market distribution. Some government agencies, where records had to be kept for over 100 years by law, were skeptical. Some sources were quoting the shelf life of CD-ROMs as only ten years. All this went through my mind as I tried to figure out what was going on.

We had changed a lot on the disc since the last update. Our policy was to have libraries send back the old discs when they received the updated ones, which meant the stricken libraries had no backup discs on-site. We quickly decided to return their old discs with a letter of apology to buy some time. The problem discs had all gone bad within a week of each other, about 30 days after going out to the libraries. That meant that the old disc we were sending back was really out-of-date.

Dion Lowery was responsible for some gray areas in NewsBank that didn't fit into one functional area or another. He knew NewsBank inside out, having worked there for several years before taking off on an extended European vacation, then returning. He was a NewsBank favorite son. He was just taking over customer support, and so we sat down to talk.

"What did we do wrong?" he asked with an air of relief (at least we had some time to try to figure out what made 50 out of 50 computers go bad). By now we had sent the old discs out, and they worked fine, so we knew almost certainly that the problem was with the disc. As I sat back in his oversized guest's chair, I looked out of the half of the window not covered by snow. Chester, Vermont was quite a place to have our production facilities, I thought, and Dion was lucky to be living there. Who would've thought decades earlier, this would be the building where microprint was pioneered—putting documents in extremely small print to be read in a similar manner as microfiche, except with microprint it looked more like a miniature post card.

"Let's see," I said. "We put in that new feature for searching by state, we had a slightly different indexing process, and we put in some new headings." I thought about it for awhile. "And then there's Vermont T's," I said.

As I said this, we looked at each other as though we could read each other's minds. It couldn't be, we thought, it just couldn't be. We both managed a small smile and I felt like we would both leap out of our chairs at any moment and run straight down to Vermont T's.

"My God," I said. "I'll bet that's it."

Vermont T's is a T-shirt silkscreening operation on the main street of Chester. They sell T-shirts with such things as "Cowabunga" and "Let's do it" written on the front, complete with pictures of half-crazed skiers bombing down the hill. Since Chester was near many of Vermont's best ski areas, Vermont T's was quite popular. If you want a t-shirt that says, "My parents went skiing in Vermont and this is all I got," then Vermont T's is the place.

They were, I'm certain, the first silkscreening company to ever use its silkscreening process to put artwork on a CD-ROM. The first time they'd done it had been on the problem discs we'd just gotten back from our customers. We grabbed our coats and headed for Vermont T's.

It didn't seem possible that it could be the art that was printed on the disc—we had checked it out thoroughly before we did it. I had talked with the owner of Vermont T's and with 3M, the only place in the U.S. that made CD-ROM discs—they said it would work if we used a certain ink. Vermont T's ordered the ink and silkscreened the NewsBank name on the discs, saving us money on production.

Dion and I reached Vermont T's, and called the engineer at 3M who had instructed us about the ink. With a certain infuriating calmness, he said, "Under what conditions was the ink administered?" Oh, I thought sarcastically, he forgot to leave out one little thing. Gee, I expected him to say, "Does Vermont T's have a 'clean room'?"

We sent the discs back to 3M for their analysis, and it was the ink. The ink had eaten through the disc—the 3M man told us to hold it up to the light. Sure enough, you could see tiny specks of light coming through where the disc had corroded.

It wasn't that we didn't want the factory to put the artwork on the disc—it was that we were sharing the disc with another company to save costs. (...meaning that both of us had data on the disc, but no one knew that but 3M and us.) One condition of doing this was the other company, the Library Corporation, put its name on its discs, and then ordered discs with no artwork for us. The factory would not allow us to split an order for two different-looking discs. After all, they were charging almost $10,000 for each master, and in this case Library Corporation and NewsBank were splitting that cost.

The Library Corporation was run by Brower Murphy (Murph), who was an entrepreneur, gadfly, businessman and computer nerd all in one package. Murph and NewsBank had a special relationship, and were horse-trading just about everything: hardware, software, and the "real estate" on the disc. He was the first person to have the CD-ROM industry "wired." He knew his way around CD-ROM drives, mastering facilities, and the industry infrastructure—which didn't even really exist except in his imaginative mind. If you needed something to do with CD-ROM, Brower could get it for you.

"Murph" does have one thing that no one can ever take away from him, and as the history of CD-ROM keeps getting rewritten to suit corporate objectives, undoubtedly some will leave him out. He was the first person to ever publish a CD-ROM product—in late 1984. He sold the first system at the American Library Association conference in January 1985. He did it with sweat, guts, and determination, after trying to get other companies to do it and being rejected. His West Virginia smarts beat Silicon Valley, Hollywood, and New York to the punch. The barn in his backyard should be declared a National Historic Monument.

Whether on purpose or not, 3M and Vermont T's had effectively broken up the Brower Murphy-NewsBank relationship. From then on, we decided to play it straight and deal directly with 3M—no disc sharing, and hopefully no see-through discs.

# six

## A Pimple on an Elephant's Ass
## 1987

I LEFT NEWSBANK BECAUSE THE CD-ROM DEVELOPMENT was over, and I wanted to pursue more activity with new CD-ROM products. Back in the Bay Area, I looked for a job—with two resumes. One emphasized my experience in CD-ROM, and the other painted me more as a generalist in the information business. Not surprisingly, most resumes I sent out were not the CD-ROM ones, although the word CD-ROM still appeared in places.

I noticed a change in people's awareness of CD-ROM since I had left to go to back East. More people were talking about it, and I heard about more varied uses, more creative ideas, and products that were outside the library market. In Sacramento, my brother Rich mentioned there was someone he wanted me to meet, someone who was in the computer

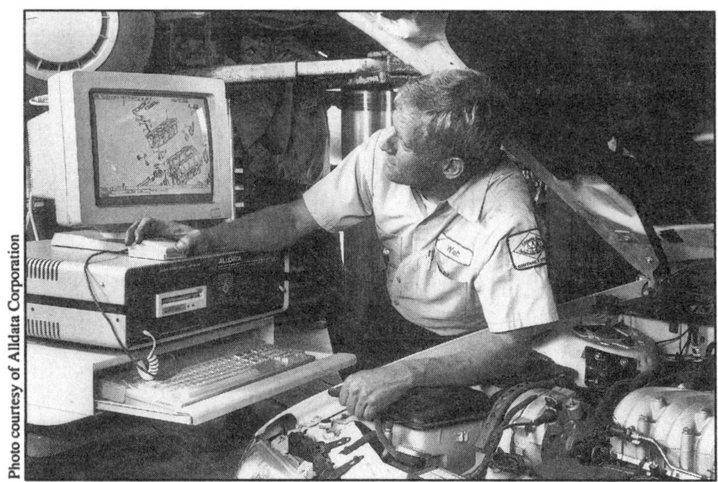

Photo courtesy of Alldata Corporation

*"Walt" at the Triple A uses the Alldata automotive information system to identify and select car parts. Alldata built its own custom cabinet to protect the CD-ROM from "grease and grime."*

business. As a tennis pro, he taught many kinds of people, and I wasn't wildly enthusiastic about meeting another tennis-playing computer executive.

I headed to the tennis court anyway, and Rich introduced me to someone who said he made CD-ROM products for automobile mechanics. His name was Rod Georgiu and the next week I paid him a visit at his office. What I saw opened my eyes to a whole new arena for CD-ROM. There was about one hundred feet of shelf space filled with automotive manuals, the ones mechanics look through to find parts, diagnose problems, and fix cars. He told me these manuals were all on a CD-ROM, which sat inside a specially-built case so mechanics could use the product directly. He then showed me a dark-gray box from which he started printing diagrams and explanations of parts. Then, he said, they could order the parts directly from an online system. The company, Alldata Corporation, had been funded through venture capital. CD-ROM, he explained, was really just a means to an end, and his first love was cars. CD-ROM was just the only thing he could find which would do what he wanted to do with these repair manuals, since his plans called for collecting and selling several hundred thousand pages of these manuals.

It was the first company I had ever seen whose sole business was CD-ROM. All the companies I had worked for pursued CD-ROM only as an extension of an existing business. I was also impressed that he hired people in the automotive business, instead of information professionals, though this dimmed my prospects of working there. Besides hiring non-information professionals, he also sold to non-information professionals: garage mechanics. With the CD-ROM, they didn't have to worry about organizing the numerous service bulletins that came each month on paper from the car manufacturer, because they were already on the CD-ROM. This reduced the risk, for example, of a manufacturer trying to inform a mechanic about a defect and the mechanic not getting vital information because of a paper overload. Alldata consolidated all those updates, put them on a disc, and sent the disc regularly to the mechanic. As well, the mechanic could print out an estimate, part description, and even a picture of a part, all for the customer—a far cry from getting a cryptic handwritten work estimate. I left Alldata with a strong sense that CD-ROM was taking on a life of its own, outside of libraries.

At one point I thought I'd landed a job with Amdek, a relative newcomer to CD-ROM who had just produced a CD-ROM drive. Thinking that Amdek "just had to get everything approved" as they put it, I began to plan a daily commute to San Jose. But when I called the man who had offered me the job, I could never reach him, and he never returned my calls. After a week of frustration, I wrote a nasty letter, and still never heard, so of course I had to conclude I didn't have the job. It was my first experience in the difference between getting a job and having a job.

I answered many ads, and one Sunday a soft-spoken man from Hewlett-Packard called. My generic resume was on his desk, but the word CD-ROM had jumped out at him—he wanted to know if I was interested in a job in CD-ROM at HP. Several interviews later, I was working at HP for Phil Palmintere.

It was obvious from the first day that I was not like the rest of the people at HP. In this extended family of product managers, marketing managers, product marketing managers, and group product marketing managers, I was the only one without an MBA. But, I was also the only one with CD-ROM experience, which became clear when they sent me to Sacramento on my second day of work to give a speech on CD-ROM at a conference of HP customers.

The first week, I was also invited to demonstrate LaserROM at the quarterly financial analysts review. John Young, the president of HP, gave a talk to the financial press about the state of HP, and after the meeting, LaserROM was one of only two products being demonstrated—out of tens of thousands of HP products.

LaserROM was new to me after the practical world of libraries. LaserROM ran under Microsoft Windows, and included graphics. Words like "pan" and "zoom" and "vector" and "raster" were used to describe the product. It was an impressive achievement, containing all the information owners of HP3000 computers needed to answer questions about their computer. And LaserROM used a mouse.

LaserROM was still a few months from completion when we showed it at the financial meeting. John Young stopped by and was very friendly, asking how things were going. I was excited to show him LaserROM and asked him if he'd like to see it. He said he had a minute so I launched into a demonstration when, much to my surprise, I could not get the little arrow to click on the thing I wanted. I'd get real close when suddenly the arrow would move away from the item I was trying to click on. I looked around for the engineer, but of course, he was gone.

I could not click on anything and had a sick feeling. I started to describe the screen, and tell him what was on the disc, but I couldn't show anything but this single screen. I kept trying, getting near to clicking on something, and the arrow would quickly move away. After Young left, the engineer came back and demonstrated the product to the press with no problems. I couldn't figure it out.

After the meeting, I got back to my cubicle, turned on my computer, and it worked fine. I kept looking at the computer—the screen—the mouse. The mouse—it must have something to do with the mouse. I turned the mouse around so it was backward—sure enough I couldn't click on anything. With the mouse turned around, I'd move the mouse to the right, but the arrow would go right, making it impossible to reach something on the screen. I had never used a mouse before coming to HP. I wondered if anyone else among the 80,000 HP employees had a mouse initiation like mine.

Cubicles and conference rooms are second nature to most Silicon Valley workers, but they took some getting used to. Cubicles are the ultimate in contradiction: "private" areas where you just have to lift yourself slightly from your chair, and you're right in your neighbor's face. They were designed to propagate peer pressure. At HP, cubicles were not just a functional design feature, they were part of the corporate culture—all the way up to the most senior levels.

HP also had a "right way" to do things. There was a right way to develop a product, outlined on a huge poster hanging in many cubicles. There was a right way to review someone's job performance, detailed with a ten-page numeric scoring system. And there were many people who knew how to do these right

*Doug Iles managed the development of CD-ROM products at HP, and built an automated production process for information. Here he is using a premastering system from Meridian Data to simulate LaserROM on a hard disk, prior to shipping it to the factory to press CD-ROMs.*

things—the right way. They called it the HP way. They were all highly-trained, and worked well as a team to produce beautifully planned products. I was used to making CD-ROMs with just myself and a programmer. I treated CD-ROM like a two-man wrestling team, whereas HP approached CD-ROM like an 11-man football team with a game plan.

I didn't feel like one of them. Not feeling comfortable at the assortment of meetings, reviews and koffee klatches, I excelled in the only way I knew how: writing. Within 60 days of arriving at HP, I developed a 50-page written plan, and promptly distributed it among the ruling class.

The plan outlined a new product named LaserRetrieve—HP LaserRetrieve was its trade name. HP LaserRetrieve was a

CD-ROM authoring system, which meant that it was software that enabled other companies to build their own CD-ROMs.

HP was just delivering LaserROM, which contained the thousands of pages of documentation for the HP-3000 minicomputer. With LaserROM, all those manuals would be instantly searchable, ultimately making the customer more self-supportive, at a lower cost to HP than delivering this information on paper. LaserROM was hailed as the first customer support CD-ROM. LaserRetrieve was born out of LaserROM.

Phil Palmintere ran the CD-ROM activities from the marketing side, along with a crusty and personable Englishman, Doug Iles, who handled R&D and product development. Marketing and R&D were in constant conflict, and Phil was usually in the middle of it. Running the entire division for HP was a man named Marc Hoff. Marc Hoff, who ran a billion dollars in business, had the fever—he had CD-ROM fever.

*Marc Hoff ran a billion dollar division for Hewlett-Packard, but what enamored him the most was CD-ROM. Here he is in front of the HP/UX manuals, all which were put on LaserROM, HP's customer support CD-ROM. Mr. Hoff died in 1992.*

Iles liked to talk about an "automated information publishing environment" to describe how HP viewed the process of CD-ROM publishing. Iles was pioneering a new concept of treating the information publishing environment as a manufacturing process that included raw materials, engineering processes, and automated systems. He talked about building an assembly line for information.

It made sense that at HP, with its engineering emphasis, they would find a way to fit the hazy idea of information into their other manufacturing processes. The numbers discussed at HP for CD-ROM were astronomical by my experience. They were talking about putting hundreds of thousands of pages on CD-ROMs, using budgets of many millions of dollars. What's more, they wanted to build all kinds of things like internal support services and corporate document publishing systems, and to publish things that had previously been on their internal mainframe.

"User documentation has existed here in a huge number of formats," Iles would say of the challenges he faced in transforming that documentation into a CD-ROM. "Most of the technical documentation HP has to prepare is available in platform-specific word-processor formats. Our challenge is to take manuals and data of all these different types and convert them to a consistent format."

Iles chose to build a system for information management, automated formatting, and language translation of the documents based on the international standard, Standard Generalized Mark-Up Language (SGML). SGML is a standard that many companies were adopting that allows for different output (paper, computer screen, etc.) from the same file. It gave the publisher the tools to produce a CD-ROM with a consistent style, look-and-feel and organization, giving the customer one place to look for support information. The process of converting the documents can be both manual and automated. Paper documents, even if they are on a computer, have to have a process for getting into the right format for CD-ROM.

I liked to do battle with Iles because he thought I was too narrow-minded. He thought of CD-ROM as it fit into the big picture, and I was a specialist. He liked to note the futility of having a "CD-ROM trade show," by saying that there were no trade shows for floppy disks.

Making CD-ROM products in the same division that handled HP's support services didn't really make sense. However, many people in the division wanted to be part of a CD-ROM product to further their careers, because they saw the high profile for such CD-ROM products. Marc Hoff seemed to approach CD-ROM as something that could raise the stock of his division within HP, and ultimately raise the profile of HP in the outside world.

But since the CD-ROM products could never generate the revenue he was used to, there was one thing he was determined to get out of it: P.R. Behind the public relations was a humorous, insightful man, not much taller than the edge of a cubicle, named Lou Hoffman. When Lou interviewed to represent HP's public relations business, he dropped off a thick stack of articles about CD-ROM for me to read. I was impressed that he was organized enough to collect these articles from such diverse publications, but even more impressed when I found out that he had ghost-written them all.

Lou was a one-man shop, and had handled the introduction of the first CD-ROM drive in the United States for Philips. At HP, he was now handling the introduction of the first technical documentation or customer support CD-ROM. He did it with ease and elegance, and created a magnet for CD-ROM within HP. Because of his work, the press profile of HP's CD-ROM activities were on par with other established, "sexier" HP businesses like high-speed computers, laser printers, and modeling software.

After I had been at HP for a while, Phil mentioned at lunch one day that someone had left HP to work for a CD-ROM company. Her name was Shelley Harrison. She had apparently been dissatisfied with the bureaucracy at HP, and had received a huge increase in salary in this job move. He was telling me in an oblique fashion that the reason there was a job available for me was because she had left. As he finished this story, I got curious.

"Where'd she go?" I asked Phil.

"Amdek," he replied. Oh, well, so at least in an indirect way, Amdek gave me a job.

I began to learn the ropes at HP and it became clear I was the specialist. I had the oddball product that didn't quite fit with the other things HP was doing, and I was supposed to figure out how to make it work. HP LaserRetrieve was CD-ROM authoring software in a world of HP 3000s, HP 9000s, manuals, software, and documentation.

The person who had the golden product, LaserROM, was Scott Fallon. Scott was a highly-charged and fast-moving worker, flying around the country to drum up support for his new CD-ROM. Every morning I'd come in, sit down, and see the last couple inches of the top of his head, bent over writing yet another document. There was the document to plan for LaserROM's implementation, the support document, the marketing pieces, and speeches. He was able to run meetings effectively and pull all the people involved with LaserROM together. He and I spoke a lot about LaserROM and LaserRetrieve, but something that was symbolic of our respective projects was the way we chose our dogs. He had two dogs that he and his wife had selected after looking through books, making sure they each got a purebred that matched their personality. My wife, Veronica, and I, on the other hand, had a couple of mutts, one we found in the back room of a copy shop, and the other one we found on the beach. Authoring software, and HP LaserRetrieve, were the mutts within HP.

Authoring software for CD-ROM is one of the most confusing aspects of the industry for people who are just getting into CD-ROM. It looks just like any other software, a few floppy disks, some manuals—or, if they have their act together, the software is actually delivered on a CD-ROM. It looks like any other software, that is, until you get out your checkbook.

Authoring software traditionally is expensive, and is one of the biggest roadblocks in CD-ROM development. Prices range from $500 to $250,000, and often it is difficult to assess the differences between the options and price ranges. On top of that, it is usually poorly documented, needs an engineer or skilled programmer to use it, and is constantly being updated to produce new versions as customers ask for more features. About 100 companies sell CD-ROM authoring software.

HP LaserRetrieve was supposed to solve some, but not all, of these problems. The main feature of HP LaserRetrieve was that it required very little time or skill to build a new CD-ROM product. If you followed certain rules, it would come out the other end looking very much like LaserROM—its great aunt. The idea was simple: limit the options of the CD-ROM publisher in exchange for simplicity and speed of development. Make everything look like LaserROM, except with different information inside the software.

Some good products have come to market in this fashion, but more often than not, this idea has failed in the CD-ROM business. Trying to develop a generalized tool for producing CD-ROM discs so that "anyone can do it," has caused some miserable failures. But I had the ultimate security screen at HP—a team of MBAs positioned to poke holes in my plan, which projected $12 million in revenues in a relatively short time. This revenue would be paid by people who would license HP LaserRetrieve and pay a royalty based on their choice of payment plans. These payment plans fell into the same trap as other authoring software: they were as complicated to understand as the software.

The different ways in which a CD-ROM publisher can choose to pay royalties for authoring software include: by number of discs pressed or sold, by annual subscription, as a percentage of revenue, by committing to a certain number of copies up-front, or as a one-time fee. On top of that, most companies in this business are hungry, resulting in a buyer's market in which deals are made that don't bear any resemblance to standard price lists.

My 50-page plan in hand, I confidently attended the review meeting that would determine if the project would get a green light. Everyone was in the room: Palmintere, Iles, Hoff, and others like Scott Fallon who headed the LaserROM project, Ann Livermore, the head of development, and Doug Chapin, a marketing manager. Hoff was seated in the corner, and heard presentations by me and the managers backing the project. Every competitor, scenario, feature, and project timeline was in the plan and there were cross-references from one section to another. After watching this show, Hoff cleared his throat.

"It's a pimple on an elephant's ass," he said sarcastically, causing lots of silent gasps in the room. My boss and his boss quickly jumped on Hoff, citing all the research and telling him we felt confident we could reach the $12 million revenue goal. A couple minutes passed, and Hoff just shook his head back and forth.

I looked at Iles, wondering if he'd be supportive or not. He had always had trouble seeing where LaserRetrieve would fit into HP's business, and liked to taunt me with his trademark comment, "They don't have trade shows for floppy disks..."

Hoff smiled. "I said it was a pimple on an elephant's ass. I didn't say we weren't going to do it."

Thus was born HP LaserRetrieve.

# seven

# Meridian Data—The First Church of CD-ROM 1988

HP LaserRetrieve got off the ground and I raised a few eyebrows when we signed a large contract with a company named Meridian Data. Meridian Data would purchase HP LaserRetrieve and package it with some of their products. What no one at HP knew is that less than five minutes after signing the contract, I was asked a question by the chairman of the board of Meridian, over lunch at the 94th Aero Squadron in San Jose.

"Are you interested in a job?" he said.

On my next-to-last day at HP, as a representative of HP, I gave a speech about HP LaserRetrieve at the Meridian Users Group meeting. In the crowd, I could see the Meridian people with slight smiles on their faces knowing I was coming to their company. And then there were the HP people, slight smiles on their faces knowing I was representing an HP product that was generating revenue. I felt hypocritical, and there was nothing I could do about it. After the speech, I quickly left by a side door and drove home.

The next morning I got to HP early, and my new boss, Doug Chapin, appeared in his cubicle a few minutes before 8:00. I walked over, asked him if he had a minute, and sat down.

"I'm leaving HP," I said.

He waited a few seconds, and I could see his anger rise to the surface. His face went dead and he looked me in the eye. I had trouble looking back.

"Meridian, right?"

Yes, I answered.

"I knew it," he said. "Follow me."

CD-ROM had always kept me in the eye of a storm. I suddenly felt like a non-person, as Chapin walked swiftly with me into Personnel. When we got there, he curtly told me to sit.

"We have someone who needs to be walked out," I heard him say to the personnel manager. When asked if I was going to a competitor, Chapin answered no, that it was a complicated situation. Next, I heard him on the phone, asking, "Where's Hoff?" After a pause, he snapped, "Find him." When he came out of the office, he was slightly calmer, and he told the lady he didn't need a guard. He'd walk me out himself.

We were walking quickly toward the door, down the long majestic hallways of HP. I remembered the old Mayfield Mall, before HP turned it into the "Mayfield Site." Gone were the pet store, J.C. Penney, and Cost Plus. During that walk, Chapin managed to get in a few digs about going to Meridian Data. If nothing else, he wanted me to feel bad. I have never met anyone who left HP who was not made to feel bad.

"Have you heard of the Bowmar Brain?" he asked me, as we moved toward the glass door. I would've given anything right then to turn that building back into Cost Plus, and be leaving the store with some tea or candles. I told him I hadn't heard of the Bowmar Brain.

"Exactly my point. Bowmar Brain was the first wrist calculator. It was about this size," he said, pretending he was holding a large navel orange. "Meridian Data is the Bowmar Brain of CD-ROM."

I understood what he was telling me. Beneath all the hate was some reason. He was saying that Meridian Data was a flash in the pan and he was disappointed I didn't see that. Meridian would be gone some day, and sometime in the 21st century a manager at HP would be walking my grandchild out the door asking, "Have you ever heard of Meridian Data?" At least I'll be able to give my grandchild some advice on how to answer that question. I walked out alone, went home, and fell asleep for several hours out of sheer exhaustion.

If you worked for Meridian Data in the late '80s, you were cool. You were hip. Meridian was a very tiny company with an extremely big presence in the CD-ROM industry. It seemed as if every major announcement in CD-ROM involved Meridian Data. Part rebel, part industry leader, part corporate kiss-ass, everyone had an opinion of Meridian Data, whether they worked for the company or not.

Meridian's main product was CD Publisher. It had been introduced in 1986, and about three-quarters of the world's CD-ROM producers used CD Publisher to build their CD-ROMs. As the salespeople at Meridian used to say, "If you want to be a player, you need to step up to a CD Publisher." Building on the fear that most people had about making their own CD-ROM, that sales tactic worked superbly.

CD Publisher was deceptively simple: it was a large hard disk with some software for formatting a CD-ROM before sending it to the factory for pressing. It debuted in 1986, giving CD-ROM

Photo by Dean Quarnstrom

*Fred Meyer, left, was the president and Michael Prussian, right, the chairman of the board of Meridian Data.*

publishers the ability to become "in-house publishers." It included an assortment of utilities and hardware that would be helpful to a CD-ROM publisher, like a nine-track tape drive so that when your CD-ROM information was the way you wanted it on a hard disk, you could copy it on tape to send to the factory. It was big and bulky and looked more like a washing machine than anything high-tech. It was sold as a "desktop" CD-ROM publishing product. What was on your desk, though, was a computer. The computer was hooked up to the 300-pound CD Publisher that sat next to your desk. One of Meridian's ad campaigns made fun of this, and showed a box of Tide sitting on a CD Publisher. That campaign was symbolic of not only the size of the product, but the attitude of the company.

My job seemed like an ideal job. As director of marketing, I was the one who had the most fun—traveling, giving speeches, going to trade shows, getting quoted in magazines, and just being cool. I felt like I was coming into my own. I made an effort to be the person on the management level who related to and cared about the company's non-management workers, many of whom were having trouble keeping up with the frantic pace of the company. Making only few million dollars a year in revenue, when the world thinks you're an industry leader, has its downside. You have to work extra hard to keep that image in people's minds with endless meetings, presentations, press releases, press tours, speeches, and seminars.

My third week on the job, I made my first trip overseas to give a speech in London. I arrived late the evening before and was disoriented from lack of sleep. Nevertheless, I spoke about CD-ROM authoring to a group of British people hungry to know what was happening in the United States. Between sessions, I met for the first time with Patrick Gibbins, the respectable and dynamic president of Pergamon Compact Solution. That night I flew back to California—my first trip to London, and I was gone the same day I came. It was a fast pace, and I began to feel more like a politician than an evangelist or a technoid. That made the speeches easier, though, since I kept repeating the same emotional themes about putting the power of CD-ROM to work. The charts, graphs, and testimonials about CD-ROM being umpteen times more efficient than other ways to distribute large amounts of information didn't hurt the cause.

Our "CD-ROM Developer's Seminar" series became very popular. It was sponsored by Meridian and a CD-ROM mastering facility named PDO. This one-day seminar about how to make a CD-ROM traveled around the U.S., drawing about 100 people to each session. It was curious that none of the speakers were publishers, but instead were suppliers of products and services targeted to CD-ROM publishers. That was consistent with the CD-ROM industry at the time, and would be equivalent to the makers of printing presses telling book publishers how to write a good book. No statistics were available, but it began to feel like 100 percent of potential CD-ROM publishers would call Meridian Data, and most would buy the product. We seemed to know everything that was going on in the industry. Many buyers would have attended a seminar.

I settled into my job at Meridian and met many interesting people. Rich Bowers, stopped in to tell me about an organization he was calling the OPA or Optical Publishing Association. They were going to have their first meeting, and would Meridian become a member? OPA, he said, was going to be the first association representing the people in the "optical publishing" business. He'd send a newsletter, gather industry statistics, and sponsor roundtables. It was one of the few times in my life I had been really negative about an idea, and after some thinking it became clear why.

The first reason was simple. "Optical Publishing" was something only about a dozen people on the planet could really relate to, and as far as I was concerned, that term was dead. CD-ROM, with a dash in the middle, was what we did, and like it or not, it was gaining acceptance as an acronym.

Another reason his pitch disturbed me was the implications of having an association at all. It signified something I wasn't sure I wanted. It had been fun to make up the rules as we went along, answering to no one, and with no armchair quarterbacks to question our motives or goals. CD-ROM seemed to attract non-conformists, and an association made me think of conformity and rules. It meant that CD-ROM, which felt like an underground subculture, was coming to the surface. It was growing up, and I wasn't sure if I was ready for that. After all, who wants to grow up?

My wife and I finally moved "over the hill" into the town of Soquel. I was looking forward to living in Santa Cruz County, which was known for its relaxed atmosphere and liberal politics. Two days before the annual Microsoft CD-ROM conference, some friends pulled into our new driveway in a 26-foot U-Haul, ready to help us move into our new house. On the street were hundreds of people—policemen, farmers, and people with animal masks on. A policeman asked sternly, "What do you have in there?" glancing at the back of the truck. I explained that I was moving in to the house. It seems it was near Easter, and since a neighbor did research on animals, specifically rabbits, the protest group had decided to target his house. At the same time, the protest group had unknowingly given me a housewarming party, Santa Cruz style.

# eight

# A CD-ROM Bake-off in the Middle of Manhattan 1989

IT WAS MID-JANUARY, AND A RIVAL COMPANY, OPTICAL MEDIA International (OMI), made an announcement that stunned the management of Meridian Data. They announced they were the first company to build a recordable CD-ROM device, and were having a press conference to demonstrate the technology. They had tested it in Japan several months before, and were going to show a working model for the first time in the United States.

The idea was simple. In traditional CD-ROM publishing, the eventual CD-ROM is tested, simulated, and prototyped on a large computer hard disk. When everything on the hard disk is exactly the way the publisher wants it, then the information is copied onto a nine-track tape (or shipped on the hard disk) to the CD-ROM factory.

With a recordable CD, also known as a writable CD or a "one-off," publishers could make their own CDs. To people who published CD-ROMs, this was the most important advancement in CD-ROM publishing imaginable. It meant the creative and development process could incorporate making a CD, instead of shipping everything to a factory just to make one for testing.

We scrambled when we realized we had been upstaged by a competitor with an announcement that signaled a significant technological advance in CD-ROM. There were varying opinions of the potential sales of these devices. But everyone agreed that it was a great story and "making your own CD" was sure to attract a lot of press attention. We decided we needed to organize our own press conference, and where else would you want to show how to make your own CD, but in the middle of New York City.

We examined the announcement from OMI with a fine tooth comb, looking for areas they might have missed. There was bad blood anyway between OMI and Meridian, and the threat of lawsuits between the two companies were commonplace. OMI would characterize Meridian as a bunch of thugs, and Meridian liked to imply that OMI was always on the verge of going out of business. They sounded like two kids fighting in a sandbox. "I'm going to be the leader!" "No, I'm going to be the leader!" This attitude was pervasive at trade shows, when each company would send spies to the other's booth to see what they were saying. The problem was, everyone knew who worked for the two companies, so rarely did the scouting produce anything more than good drama.

The president of OMI was Allen Adkins. Yes, the same Allen Adkins who five years earlier had given me his flow chart in a schoolroom in Mountain View. Adkins sold his first premastering system in 1986 to Sonopress, part of the German publishing giant Bertelsmann. The same year, Meridian sold its first system to Triad, a large automotive parts distributor. Since then, OMI and Meridian had become the only two companies in the

CD-ROM premastering business in the U.S., except for Reference Technology who sold a system made by a European company. Coincidentally, both Meridian and OMI had begun business near Santa Cruz, California.

In the Macintosh and music arenas, OMI was considered more creative and knowledgeable. In the technical documentation and database area, which was the bulk of the CD-ROM business, Meridian was ahead. In the presidential image department, Fred Meyer liked to view himself as an astute visionary, leading from a distance but not touching. Adkins' image was as I had seen him years earlier, an "on-the-leading-edge" inventor who would break new ground, then not quite be able to take advantage of his pioneering effort. The recordable CD was no exception.

Moving with precision and speed, Lou Hoffman organized a press conference in New York City. Lou handled the PR for Meridian Data as well as HP, which put him in an awkward position when I left HP. We hoped that the Optical Media announcement would not make much noise. As Lou said, "If a tree falls in the forest, and no one is around to hear, did it make a sound?" Luckily, OMI's press conference on January 31 didn't make much noise, and we had the benefit of hearing several informal reports about their demonstration. We thought we might have a hit by playing up "the first time a CD is going to be made in the middle of New York City." Who could resist?

We found a comrade in Rick Doherty, a respected writer who happened to have the world's largest private collection of information on the Challenger shuttle disaster. He had known the late Dr. Richard Feynman, the respected Nobel prize winner who testified at the Challenger hearings, and had collected information from the hearings in his memory. He had all the transcripts from the hearings, in text and on tape. What better demonstration for the press, we decided, than to type in "o-ring" and find the testi-

*The CD Professional from Meridian Data, one of the first systems which gave CD-ROM publishers the ability to make their own discs.*

mony where Dr. Feynman made his famous demonstration in front of Congress. The audience could hear his speech right off the disc. Plus, we would make this disc right on the spot. We were certain this would be the first time any of the audience would have seen a CD being made.

It was exciting to see who accepted the invitation to the press conference—*Rolling Stone*, *TIME*, *Business Week*, *New York Times*. We boarded the plane for New York, with most of our fears now centered on how to get 600 pounds of equipment to the hotel and guarantee that it worked. Working against us were the three weeks it took for our technical people to build "CD Professional." Working for us was the fact that it was essentially an integration of the Yamaha CD Recorder with the Meridian

CD Master, which was an advanced version of the CD Publisher for mastering facilities, so it required little original development.

Arriving at the hotel, we found the union men uncrating two big boxes. Scott, the Meridian engineer, quickly went to work setting up the system. We decided to put the CD Professional on the opposite side of the room from where we would play the finished disc, emphasizing that we were really making a disc and not faking it. Fred Meyer and I would give the speeches. I would concentrate on the nuts and bolts, and make the disc during my talk. I'd start by describing the CD Professional, then make the Challenger disc—which would be finished ten minutes and ten megabytes later. Fortunately, we decided to scrap our oven mitt idea, and the whole idea of "baking the disc." Humor would have been pushing it.

After the demonstration, Fred would give his high-level talk, and answer questions. The question we dreaded was, "What is different between this announcement and the OMI announcement?" We practiced our speeches well into the night, with the help of Bob Callaway, a colleague of mine from NewsBank and a speech coach. Bob worked on many things that were not new to me, since I had spent a lot of time with him. On the other hand, Fred was enthusiastic about working on his speech, but he didn't pick up the physical, visual style Callaway preached. Fred, always the professor, was attached to his charts, graphs, and calm, deliberate hands. Callaway went for image and results and personality. Maybe we should've just left Fred alone. Fred's hands took on an appearance of a confused kitten, not sure where to go or what to do.

The next day, March 21, 1989, we made a CD-ROM for the first time in New York in front of 50 press people. I placed a blank $100 Fuji disc into the CD Professional, and started the process. I talked for nine minutes, then the drawer popped out and the disc was done. I carried it over to the computer with the CD-ROM drive, Scott put the disc in and typed "Russian roulette." From the 17,000 pages appeared a quotation by Dr. Feynman about NASA's statistical overconfidence, comparing it to Russian roulette. Next, the room was filled with the sound of Dr. Feynman speaking the same words—from the same disc. I could see the eyes of the reporters looking around the computer wondering if our demonstration was for real. Fred then gave his speech. The question of OMI and Meridian did come up, and Fred handled it elegantly. The whole thing came off without a hitch.

Whether we convinced these people that we were showing something revolutionary remained a question. There was no doubt though, that they thought it was pretty neat to see a CD-ROM being made, especially one that had 17,000 pages of information and audio from the Challenger hearings. And all in ten minutes. In the following weeks, the CD Professional was everywhere, including in *Business Week* where it was portrayed somewhat tongue-in-cheek as a "way for little guys to make CDs on desktops...a do-it-yourself desktop discmaker," costing only $98,000. At 600 pounds, that's only $166 a pound—a bargain.

# nine

## Pow! Wham! Let's Have Lunch
## 1989

IT WAS A FRIDAY, NOT UNLIKE ANY OTHER FRIDAY AT Meridian Data. I had been there six months, and we had been in our new building barely a week. It was in Scotts Valley, California, the high-tech center of Santa Cruz County. We had just posted our best month ever, due to the CD Professional catching on at $100K apiece. Large corporations were the big buyers, using it for their internal publishing of documents. Hewlett-Packard and Apple Computer were two of the first customers, giving the technology a much-needed level of respectability.

I was organizing my office and unpacking some papers from the move. If I had been really perceptive, I would've noticed something was wrong with the size of my new office quarters. It was about half the size of the offices of two people who worked for me. I reasoned that I probably had a better location, and took pride that I wasn't the kind of guy to complain about things like that.

My intercom buzzed. "Can you come in here for a minute?" It was Fred. I walked to the other side of the building and found Fred and Michael waiting for me.

"Have a seat," Fred invited.

Following exactly on cue, Michael Prussian, chairman of the board of Meridian Data peered up from his slouching position and said, "We're letting you go."

"What?" I gasped.

"It's just not working out," he said. Fred sat silently, staring at his desk, with his hands in their usual "spider doing push-ups in a mirror" configuration.

I could feel myself start to explode, and had no control over my thoughts. The past six months flashed through my mind...recruited by them, left a good job, sold my house, they just had their best quarter, my wife now drives 100 miles a day. I just got here. What's going on?

The rest of the conversation was short and tense. I could get nothing more out of them. In a state of shock, I went back to my office, repacked my things, and went home. I remember stopping by their office on the way out, and trying to get an answer out of them one more time. They had only blank stares and shoulder shrugs.

Over the weekend, my mind went wild. What had I done to get fired? What was I going to do? Was I angry, depressed, or what? I also got on the phone to an old lawyer friend of mine and asked him if I had any legal rights. He didn't know all the details, but agreed to get back to me.

Monday I woke up to the sound of the phone ringing. I assumed it was another person calling me to ask, "What happened?"

"Can you have lunch today?" asked my caller. It wasn't a well-wisher or a sympathizer. It was Prussian.

"Why?" I asked, with an obvious anger in my voice.

"I just wanna have lunch and talk about some things," he replied. "Can you be at the Chaminade at noon?"

"Okay, fine," I ended the conversation.

I called my lawyer friend and told him what happened. Why would Prussian be asking me to lunch right after firing me?

He knew exactly what to do. "We've gotta bug you," he said. "Go talk to Paul at the office supply store and he'll show you how to do it. Make sure you've got one that you can wear easily and doesn't beep." When I asked him if it was legal to record a conversation like that, he said it was. He thought there was a very real potential that I might be offered money to keep my mouth shut, or some sort of bribe.

I had told the lawyer over the weekend where Michael Prussian's money had come from, that his family owned the largest parking lot business in Chicago. "All those lots with the capital 'P' and a down arrow were his," I had told him. "If you've been to Chicago, you'd not only recognize that sign, you'd have thought that half the city was made up of these parking lots." The Chicago angle added to the suspense around this mysterious lunch—not to mention the number of times I'd heard people say, "Don't mess with Prussian."

I rushed down to see Paul in the office supply store, and he took me into the back room to see the different options and methods. I quickly bought a "wire" that only had a slight problem—a red light that showed through the inside lining of my coat. It might be seen if I opened my coat. I said it was okay, that I'd just put adhesive tape on the light and it wouldn't shine through. This little "dictation machine" had all the other features I wanted: long-playing, no noise, and great fit.

At home, I practiced my acting skills with my wife helping me. I practiced looking "natural," and at the same time making sure I wasn't giving away anything that would make Prussian think something was fishy. I was charged up, ready to record, and left for lunch.

I drove to Chaminade a little early. The tape was only 60 minutes long, so I didn't want to start it too soon. I popped into the bathroom, into a stall, and quickly tested it. Everything checked out, so I pressed "Play" and "Record," and for the first time in my life felt like a bit player on Magnum P.I.

It couldn't have been more than minute until I literally bumped into Prussian near the hostess stand. We were seated quickly, and as the tape will acknowledge, nothing much was said until we were seated, and I said:

"Why did you ask me here?"

He looked up from the table, and half-under his breath answered, "I want to make sure we're telling the same story."

Feeling my blood boil, I stared at him. "What story is that?"

"That you left Meridian to start your own business."

I could feel my blood pressure rising and I felt like slugging him. It was the most arrogant thing I had ever heard. I then took the lawyer's advice, calmed down, and tried to get him to say some things.

"I need to know why you fired me," I said to Michael. This, apparently, was an important question from the lawyer's perspective, and he told me to keep asking it. I did just that.

Prussian and I went over lots of details, me pressing him for answers and getting none. The best answer I could get out of him was that the "chemistry wasn't right." That was a real strange comment coming from someone I had known for a long time even before they had offered me the job. We had always had tremendous success with anything we had done together. Then he said something that went right to my gut.

"Well, maybe we made a mistake." A mistake? He fired me the day before and he was telling me maybe he made a mistake?

As our talk neared 45 minutes, I wanted to change the subject because I did feel I was owed some money, if nothing else. I was also getting nervous about the tape recorder making a click when it stopped.

We talked about a number of uncomfortable subjects, then I got up and left, at just under sixty minutes. We hadn't ordered a thing, and to this day I don't know if he stayed for lunch or not.

The next week was filled with confusing activity. Listening to the tape many times, my lawyer thought we had a case. I talked to many other people, including lawyers and other victims of "wrongful termination." I found out I fit into a risky category. My protection, as a high-level employee of a small company, was not great. There was an expectation in the legal arena that I had gone into a situation like Meridian "with my eyes open." I talked to people who had sued for wrongful termination, and none had spent less than two years proving their case.

Nonetheless, all my friends urged me to sue, and the lawyer said he'd take the case on contingency. I had only two choices: either sue and devote all my time to it, or don't sue and get on with my life. I knew I couldn't sue and expect to find another job, because I would be blackballed in an industry as small as the CD-ROM one was.

I thought about my predecessor at Meridian and the things Doug Chapin said to me when I left HP. Yes, some signs had been there to "watch out for" before I joined Meridian. The previous director of marketing, an outgoing man named Mark Sheldon, left Meridian on his own accord and I never asked him why. I did know, though, what job he went to and that should've told me something. His next job was selling FishFinders. That's right, FishFinders.

I decided not to sue, and instead took occasional pleasure in letting someone else in on this story. "The tape" became well-known among certain circles. And ideas of what to do with the tape have been creative, including making a new CD-ROM product out of it, "accidentally" blasting it over the loudspeakers at a trade show, and sending Prussian a copy with an "18-minute gap" to tease his imagination.

# ten

# The Fastest Start-up in CD-ROM History
## 1989

IN 1989, LINDA HELGERSON WAS THE UNDISPUTED "QUEEN OF CD-ROM." She published *CD Data Report*, which was the only source of CD-ROM industry information in the mid-1980s. She also worked at CD-ROM as if it was a war: you were either on her side or against her.

Getting into Linda's publications was a schizophrenic experience. It is always nice to have your products or name mentioned, but you had to read whatever Linda wrote several times to read between the lines. Her publications, which later included *CD-ROM EndUser* and *DISC* magazine were nothing if not opinionated.

Home from lunch with Prussian, on my first day of being unemployed, I tried to decide what to do next. I felt totally useless, having fallen just as fast as I had risen. It was time to start my business.

Linda called that afternoon.

"What happened?" she asked.

There were about eight different ways to answer that question. Everything from "Tell her everything," to "Keep your mouth shut," went through my mind.

"You know," I finally said.

And she did know, because she had been waging war against Meridian Data, and specifically the two people who fired me, for many years. We had one three-hour phone conversation when I was at Meridian Data when I called to ask what she had against the company. (It was not difficult to tell Linda hated Meridian Data—just read any of the articles she wrote about the company.) I underlined a dozen or so references to Meridian Data in her magazine, and repeated them back to her. She had painted Meridian as a bunch of thieves. In that long conversation, Linda accused Michael and Fred of about a dozen "code violations." The vendetta, though, that she would take to her grave was over Microsoft Extensions.

Microsoft Extensions is the piece of software that allows a CD-ROM drive to communicate with a computer. Linda believed this software should be free or very inexpensive, and it sounded like she had a plan to distribute it. Meridian, on the other hand, had fashioned a product and a decent revenue stream from selling Microsoft Extensions. Meridian was making money on something that Linda thought she should be giving away.

It was a dizzying exercise to keep up with new releases of Microsoft Extensions, coupled with new releases of MS-DOS, along with varying versions of the software drivers specific to a particular drive manufacturer. This delivery system, which is more suitable to a computer hobbyist than a consumer, has plagued the CD-ROM industry since its beginning. Hardware and software people benefited from this circus, selling this software to work with that hardware, or this thing to make those other two things work. Insiders breezed through this maze, but outsiders were confronted with a confusing matrix of choices about computer type, RAM, Windows or DOS or whatever, computer speeds, CD-ROM drive access speeds, etc. "Will this work on this computer?" is not an easy question to answer.

Linda believed she was blind-sided by Michael and Fred, and that they were the reason she couldn't freely distribute Microsoft Extensions. She wasn't specific about what the Meridian people had done, but whatever it was, it was bad. In a way, Linda was way ahead of most of the industry—she was the first real end-user advocate, fighting for things that the average person who bought a CD-ROM drive would care about. At the time, though, the average person was not a great concern—typical CD-ROM products cost several hundred to several thousand dollars, and most of the business was on the high end of the market. If a customer had to make a few calls, spend $50 for the newest version of Microsoft Extensions, and get their tech person to make the product work, then so be it.

I talked to Linda, trying to make sense of my life and figure out where to go.

Linda asked, "What are you going to do?"

"I'm going to start a business," I said.

"I'm going to press today with *CD Data Report*. What kind of business?"

I told her I was going to publish CD-ROMs. When she asked me the name of my new company, I spun off a list of 10 possible names—Compact Data, Ondisc, Online Insight, UniDisc...

"That's a great name." she said. "UniDisc sounds right for what you are doing."

"OK," I said, "then we're UniDisc." What I was doing, I didn't really know, but at least I had a name. It was my first working day after leaving Meridian. It felt good to get back on my feet, and be forced to answer some questions instead of sulk. A week later my name was in *CD Data Report*, and the morning it came in the mail I received a call. Chris Bowman, vice president of marketing for KnowledgeSet asked what happened. By then I had fashioned my standard reply, "Things didn't work out."

"I saw your announcement in Helgerson's newsletter. We've got some office space here that you can rent. You can also use the fax machine and copier and the conference room, and the rest of the offices if you want."

It felt like someone had snatched me from the nether world and brought me back to the surface of the planet when he made that offer—especially since I had no time to plan, no financing, and hadn't tackled the realities of starting a business. Though it would be an hour's drive to my new offices, I said yes. We decided that we would have an informal business association, and it might benefit both businesses if we were near each other. Since my business was looking more like a consulting business, and KnowledgeSet sold software and technical services, it might just work.

I had tremendous respect for Chris Bowman, who was one of the few people I found genuinely funny in a business where most people related best to computers. A former schoolteacher, I could easily picture him waving his arms around, inspiring a group of eager students. He had a full head of gray hair, and seemed on the verge of chuckling most of the time.

KnowledgeSet was the granddaddy of CD-ROM software companies. It was founded in 1984 by Gary Kildall, a computer industry pioneer, and Tom Rolander. Tom was a top-notch technical person who always seemed to be either just starting or just ending a marathon, still in his sweats. They were originally located in Monterey, California, but gradually they moved to Mountain View, California. Now their offices occupied the fourth and fifth floors of one of the few buildings still untouched by the gentrification of Mountain View.

In the '60s and '70s, San Antonio Road created a visible and spiritual line between Palo Alto and Mountain View. Mountain View, to the south, was known more for its abundance of Chinese and Mexican restaurants, and still had the feel of the pre-Silicon Valley-era apricot orchards. Palo Alto, to the north, managed to stay consistently chic and academic, and was one of the few high-tech addresses that meant anything. If you had an office in Palo Alto, you were either one of the early pioneers, like Hewlett-Packard, or a successful consultant, like Tom Peters. As the '80s and '90s approached, real estate prices in Palo Alto skyrocketed. Mountain View seemed the obvious place to move upscale. A downtown project, with its tree-lined sidewalks and new outdoor cafes, made that a reality, and Mountain View was suddenly on the map.

KnowledgeSet was best known for its KRS software, most successfully used on the CD-ROM that contained the Boeing 767 manuals. This CD-ROM allowed users to find information, look at drawings and schematics, and replaced hundreds of pounds of paper documentation. KnowledgeSet also recently signed an agreement with Pergamon Compact Solution in the U.K., giving PCS the right to sell and distribute KnowledgeSet's software.

Several weeks after starting UniDisc, Chris Bowman came by and asked if I'd sign a non-disclosure agreement. After I did, he began to tell me about a project between KnowledgeSet and PCS. They were putting the *Guinness Book of Records*, the best-selling book in the world, on a CD-ROM. He asked me to put together a proposal that would be sent to Patrick Gibbins, president of Pergamon Compact Solution, whom I had met in London. Several weeks later, Patrick called, and I was officially the consultant/representative/advisor for the Guinness Disc of Records.

Linda Helgerson gave me a name, Chris Bowman gave me an office, and Patrick Gibbins gave me an assignment. UniDisc was looking like a business, even without business cards or a letterhead.

# eleven

# From Earthquakes to the U.S. Geological Survey 1989

It was October 17, 1989, a few minutes past five in the afternoon. I was on the phone with the office supply store—at the same time thinking about a trip I was planning in a few days to New Canaan for my high school reunion, wondering what it would be like.

Suddenly, I felt a sharp jolt and a pain in my back, and heard a scream.

"Did you feel that?" the woman asked.

"I sure did," I said. The woman on the other end of the phone and I parted quickly but politely.

Running out of my office, I saw a woman from KnowledgeSet in her leotards, terrified. "Come on, quickly," I yelled, and we ran down four flights of stairs, through dust and shaking walls. Somehow, I didn't think she was going make it to her aerobics class.

Earthquakes are a fact of life in California but there are earthquakes and there are EARTHQUAKES. Nothing can prepare you for the feeling of going through a real earthquake. It not only shakes the ground, it makes your soul quiver. The one thing you're always sure of, the ground beneath you, is suddenly not so permanent.

After waiting outside for half an hour, several of us ran back into the building to get our keys, before the building had been inspected. It's amazing how many steps you can leap in a single bound if your eyes are focused on your car keys four flights up. In hindsight, it's a great way to risk an aftershock and injury, which fortunately didn't happen.

I drove home through Cupertino, trying to call my wife from several places along the way. All the phones were out. It was nearly dark, my gas tank was low. On the main road, Highway 85, traffic moved at about three miles per hour. People were abandoning their cars on the side of the road and walking. The smell of smoke and gas was everywhere. Everyone had their windows down, exchanging information and asking questions.

"The Bay Bridge collapsed," one person said, and I felt my heart drop. I knew the World Series was on, and I imagined the panic there.

"Highway 17 is closed!" I heard a walker yell to a person in the car in front of me.

"The epicenter was somewhere between Santa Cruz and Watsonville," someone said in the car next to me. My pulse throbbed and my palms turned sweaty. Our house, that we had moved into just six months earlier, was right between Santa Cruz and Watsonville.

It was pitch dark and ten minutes later I was out of gas. I pulled to the side of the road, got out, and left the car.

"Are you going to Santa Cruz?" I asked each passing car. Sticking my thumb out was not necessary. Traffic was moving so slowly that I had time to chat with all the passersby. Finally, a woman said she was going that way and told me to hop in. Several hundred yards down the road, she pulled over again and the woman who had been in the car in front of us got out, and got into our car. She too was out of gas, and they were friends, following each other.

It was quiet except for the sound of engines running as the talkative atmosphere turned to tension and fear. Most car windows were up now, as ours was. My new friends invited me to spend the night at a house of a relative close by because it was clear we couldn't get over the mountain. We arrived at a small conservative house, and immediately found a neighbor who had a working cellular phone. Though we couldn't get through to my wife, we did reach my ride's husband on their cellular phone, and he drove the several miles to my house to let my wife know that I was okay.

Home the next morning, I listened to Veronica tell earthquake stories that made me realize it had been much worse for her than for me. There was the 100-pound dresser that flew across the room. Then there were the freak things, like the television that was exactly in the same place it had been before the earthquake, only turned 180 degrees with the back facing the room. The same happened with the large cement Buddha in the backyard. The tent was in the backyard and Veronica was proud of being so tough—even if she did end up spending the night in a neighbor's trailer.

We examined the house, and saw it was leaning to the left as you looked from the front. A crack wound around the entire house, at about the level of the floor. We took turns running into the house, quickly grabbing some clothes or valuables, and putting

*Jerry McFaul, founder of SIGCAT, the world's largest CD-ROM interest group.*

them in the car. Just before nightfall, we finished packing the car, put the dogs in the back seat, and headed to Sacramento.

Several days later, we boarded a plane for Washington, DC. I had missed my high school reunion, but I was still scheduled to talk about the economics of CD-ROM to a group named SIGCAT. The SIGCAT meeting was, coincidentally, at the U.S. Geological Survey offices in Reston, Virginia.

SIGCAT, which stands for Special Interest Group in CD-ROM Applications and Technology, is the world's largest CD-ROM interest group. They meet every couple months, usually in Reston, Virginia, the headquarters of the U.S. Geological Survey. The irony of having just experienced the earthquake, and being at the U.S. Geological Survey, was not lost as the founder of SIGCAT, Jerry McFaul, introduced me. Several years earlier, I had been taught to "clear the board" in giving a talk—which meant to handle up front any issues that might get in the way of what you are trying to say. With that in mind, I spoke briefly about what it was like to go through the earthquake. I could see by their reactions that I was something I had only seen on television, a "disaster victim."

We visited for awhile after the session, and I introduced Veronica to many people. The bonus of the earthquake was Veronica's seeing me, for the first time, make a speech. Jerry McFaul and I reminisced about how far SIGCAT had come, starting originally as a group of 30 people from different government agencies that Jerry called together in May of 1986. That the group had grown to 6,000 members in 48 countries was unimaginable.

SIGCAT was a labor of love for Jerry. He was fueled also by a tremendous need in the government to disseminate information more effectively at a lower cost. CD-ROM came to the rescue, and Jerry had many success stories to tell. A prime example was the Federal Code of Regulations sold by the Government Printing Office. As a paper product, it sold for $1800 in many volumes. Now on CD-ROM, the price was $30.

Jerry and the USGS have produced exciting CD-ROM discs that contain maps, information, and photos. The Earthquake Digital Data disc from the National Earthquake Information Center, a part of USGS, contains data for earthquakes worldwide of magnitude 5.5 or greater. Another disc contains selected earthquake data going back to 2100 BC. USGS CD-ROM projects usually have many discs to hold the tremendous detailed data available. The U.S. government's commitment to CD-ROM is underscored by the more than 200 titles originating from government agencies, and Jerry's frequent remark that at least once a week a new government application of CD-ROM crosses his desk. Jerry even takes it one step further, saying that "CD-ROM is now being used as the primary means of digital dissemination throughout the U.S. government."

The recordable CD-ROM technology also made many agencies look at CD-ROM as a possible archival medium, which looks quite good when compared to a magnetic tape. No one is quite sure how long a recordable CD-ROM will last without loss of integrity, but most agree that it will do much better than the 10-year life of a magnetic tape. As well, with the ability to not only put the data on a CD-ROM, but also supporting documentation and software, CD-ROM as an archival medium looks like it has a bright future in the government.

The government's finding practical uses for CD-ROM has been a significant reason for the technology to stay alive during the lean years. At times, 25% of the worldwide CD-ROM business, as measured by such things as sales of CD-ROM publishing systems, has been centered around Washington, DC. SIGCAT spawned not only numerous working groups to handle specific problems, but began its own conference. It was also found that CD-ROM could help in handling real issues, besides just being a substitute for another way of doing things. An example of this is the Afloat Shipping Guide, which assists Navy personnel in identifying supply items. With 100,000 marine mammals and one million birds dying each year from either ingesting or becoming entangled in plastic, this CD-ROM gives the Navy a way to find nonplastic substitutes for plastic consumables and packaging materials on board ships.

CD-ROM, with its portability, has found a friend in anyone who needs to use information in a remote location: a ship, plane, or even an agricultural research station in the most remote part of the world. Compared to carrying, and updating, large manuals which can weigh hundreds or thousands of pounds, the speed, accessibility, and lightweight of the CD-ROM make it a natural substitute for large documents. The Navy is using CD-ROM aboard ships, and organizations like the World Bank and United Nations are using CD-ROM for distribution of information to remote locations.

After the SIGCAT speech, we drove to Connecticut to have lunch with the Pembertons, Jeff, Jenny, and Adam. The

Pembertons published several magazines, including *ONLINE* and *DATABASE*, and ran one of the major conferences in the online industry. They were trying to figure out where CD-ROM fit into their business, and were considering changing the name of one of their magazines, *Laserdisk Professional*, to *CD-ROM Professional*. Their conference was coming up, and I was going to introduce a new idea there: a table where people could come by and learn how to produce their own CD-ROM. I told them I'd still make the conference.

That night, Veronica and I went out to dinner with old friends in New Canaan. It was the first time we had been with friends since the earthquake, and after many stories over drinks, I could tell that they still didn't understand how much this experience had affected us. We were shaky, unsure, and we didn't know if we had lost our house. I couldn't remember if we had signed up for earthquake insurance—a $200 decision six months earlier that had seemed insignificant. And since the computers at the local insurance company were down, they hadn't been able to tell us our status.

Harlan, my tennis buddy from high school, shook the table violently and yelled, "Earthquake!" Everyone laughed loudly, and luckily Veronica and I had had enough to drink that we laughed, too. What none of them knew, though, was that both Veronica and I really were affected by the table shaking. In fact, any shaking that occurred for several months bothered us, especially the rumble of people walking on an unsteady floor. We laughed, but when they weren't looking, we took a deep breath to relax.

There was a small amount of snow on the ground and we decided to drive to Vermont. Along the way, we debated what to do. Our business had started only a few months earlier, we were out of money, and we had a broken house. We considered moving back to the east coast, especially after hearing so many people say they "couldn't understand how we could live there knowing about the risk of earthquakes."

We drove to a small town in northern Vermont and, in the foothills along a long dirt road, found the farm I was born on. Though there was a chain along the driveway saying "No Trespassing," we parked and walked the half-mile to the farmhouse. It was abandoned, but I still recognized the layout: the pond, the apple trees, and the forest. I looked at the farmhouse, which I remembered mostly from pictures of me or people in my family sitting on the front steps. What I saw was a pile of wood, two by fours, stacked randomly with some stray pieces strewn about. I looked for significance in this ramshackle house, trying to figure out what it all meant. All I could decide was it meant it was time to move on, and I felt surprisingly refreshed. We walked back down the road, stopping to notice the health of the apple trees, and left.

We moved back to the Bay area for several months while they worked on our house. We felt lucky to miss the traffic jams on Highway 17 which turned the 40-mile trip into a three-hour one for people who had to go over the hill. Most of the deaths and tragedy occurred in San Francisco and Oakland because of the collapsed bridge and ramp, but this was definitely Santa Cruz County's earthquake. The damage to the houses in the area, especially the old Spanish houses in Watsonville, and the older office buildings in downtown Santa Cruz, was unlike anything I had ever seen. Santa Cruz had been struggling for years to figure how to make the leftist politics of the '60s jibe with the current business pressure to create an economically sound downtown. Now it had a tragic yet wonderful opportunity: since there was no longer a downtown, they could start fresh.

# twelve

# Playing the Keyboards at the Disco Techdoc

## 1990

"TECHDOC" IS SHORT FOR "TECHNICAL DOCUMENTATION," AND implies an electronic method of publishing documents. Technical documentation is one of those terms that is crystal clear to people who do these things, but from most people it draws a blank stare.

The essence of Techdoc is manuals—user manuals, procedure manuals, safety manuals, engineering manuals, how-to manuals, parts manuals. They are all books with lots of writing accompanied by drawings, charts, diagrams. They tend to be thick, usually are accompanied by related manuals about related things, and they change frequently, requiring "version control" or knowing which version is which. HP was the first company to go beyond thinking of CD-ROM as merely *storage* for technical documents, and use it instead as a publishing medium.

Stephanie Rosenbaum owned a company named Tec-Ed that specialized in producing technical documents. We had talked during the past couple years about possibly doing a seminar together for publishing managers of companies. Stephanie could handle the document production, and such issues as what fonts to use, how to lay out a page on the computer screen so it was easy to read, and human factor issues involved in putting documents on a computer instead of a book. I could then talk about the CD-ROM issues: authoring software, production, prices, design.

We produced a brochure and called the seminar "From Print to CD-ROM: A Seminar for Documentation Managers." We rented space at Rickey's Hyatt House in Palo Alto and managed to get good attendance from a wide range of companies. All the attendees had one thing in common: they were in charge of large document collections.

The big question on everyone's mind was authoring software. Should it be fixed-field or full-text? These esoteric concepts are always a barrier to people getting into CD-ROM. The best way to answer the question was to show them. Three computers were set up on the front table, and with three keyboards in front of me, I was ready to "play some mean CD-ROM." I started playing the first keyboard, which was connected to a computer with Knowledge Access software. I explained that this was fixed-field which worked well with indexes, and was suitable for library reference books. It could sort, rank, and let you make your own "sets." With Knowledge Access software, you typed in lots of "ands" and "ors," using my old friend, Boolean searching. Knowledge Access, founded by two Ph.D.s, Matilda Butler and Bill Paisley, had a reputation in the library community and had been an early entrant into the CD-ROM business.

Next, I demonstrated KnowledgeSet software, and showed them more diagrams and what looked like a user manual for a refrigerator.

It had specifications, a description, and a drawing, and was loosely put together. This was full-text software. Instead of typing in "ands," we clicked on chapter headings and looked at diagrams.

Then I switched computers and showed them some hybrid products that needed both kinds of software. We observed how it was not difficult for one type of software to mimic the other. The point was to get them to think about broadening their choices instead of just using the software like everyone else did. Visually, I tried to switch back and forth as quickly as possible to communicate these esoteric concepts that were much easier to see in action than explain. With the lights dimmed and three keyboards in front of me, I felt like I was onstage playing music, except the only sound in the room besides my voice was the click of the keyboard keys.

After Stephanie gave her talk, we broke into groups and had the participants do some role playing. This caught them by surprise, but we needed to equip them with some basic survival skills so they could champion CD-ROM in their companies once they left the class. These group exercises emphasized the personal nature of CD-ROM. One exercise asked people to pretend that they were trying to get funding for a new CD-ROM project in their company, had just submitted a proposal, and...

*The director of computer operations, who is on the executive committee, has called a meeting of systems analysts, engineers, and documentation specialists to discuss the technical implications of your proposal. The director wants to "get a handle" on the software and end-user requirements so he can discuss the CD-ROM project intelligently at the executive meeting next week.*

*You arrive at the conference room early. The director is already in his chair, riffling through some notes. His face is flushed, but he smiles at you, hands you an agenda, and motions you toward an empty seat at the table.*

*Director: Glad you could make it! Don't worry, this is the right date. The others will be along in a minute. I got here early and started picking at a few technical bones, is all.*

*You: That's fine with me. Maybe I can help dig up a few.*

*Director: Now that you mention it, maybe you can clear up a few things—just to make sure I get this straight. I gather you want to dump your whole library on CD-ROM and then use a data retrieval package to pull stuff up on a screen, right?*

*You: In a nutshell, yeah.*

*Director: And it'll have all kinds of stuff, like text and parts lists and schematics and blueprints? All that?*

*You: Yes, exactly what we have on paper now. Blueprints, too. CD-ROM can store blueprints. And we want the user to be able to call anything up to the screen fast, in a second or so. I guess I don't know what you're driving at.*

*Director: Take blueprints for starters. Blueprints aren't small. How are you going to fit one on a screen? It won't be readable.*

*You: Our retrieval software will have to handle graphics. We've been looking into several packages. But you're right—we'd probably have to modify the graphics display software.*

*Director: That could get hairy. And this other stuff too. You must have a dozen formats we'll need to get on a screen somehow. How many modifications will we have to make to vendor software? We don't want to patch good software with crazy-quilt routines. It would be a kludge.*

*You: We don't want to write our own retrieval software from scratch either. Are you saying you don't want to customize software?*

*Director: No, but patched software never works as well as the original stuff. And I'm worried that your CD-ROM library won't be too usable when you get it.*

*How do you answer the director of computer operations?*

We wanted to equip the participants with enough survival skills that they could go back to their companies and answer the typical questions. They understood that they had several choices about how they decided to make their CD-ROM. They also needed to understand the volatile nature of typical corporate CD-ROM projects. New CD-ROM projects were usually highly visible and subject to much criticism from the people who didn't want to change.

The seminar was received well except by one person who filled out the evaluation form with a scathing remark that we didn't know what we were talking about. It turned out he was the same guy who had constantly brought up questions dealing with sound and color images, which most techdoc people were not using, and he used the word multimedia a lot. He was from Apple, and as far as I was concerned, he was in the wrong class.

Techdoc found a friend in CD-ROM. Instead of sending out large books, CDs were sent that were instantly accessible. Plus, if the manual was written for a piece of software, the software itself could reside on the disc with the manual. CD-ROM was a less expensive alternative to other methods of distributing software and documents.

Cost was a driving force in many companies' CD-ROM decisions, but other benefits of using CD-ROM for software distribution included fewer manufacturing errors, ease of transport and archival, less physical space, and higher durability and reliability. Companies could streamline their software manufacturing process, delivering a higher quality product for a lower price. CD-ROM was especially well-suited for software distribution if thousands of people needed the software because of the automated, robotically-controlled manufacturing process which produced thousands of discs in days.

In my hunt for companies wanting to produce technical documents on CD-ROM, I met Sheri Loomer, who was the publications manager for Intel and responsible for a large collection of books. One collection, the candidate for CD-ROM, totaled 16,600 pages of text, diagrams, schematics, and tables.

Sheri was in a typical situation of having expertise in book and manual publishing. Suddenly, CD-ROM offered a tremendous opportunity, but she had neither the staff or time to produce her own CD-ROM product. Sheri called me as a kind of insurance, to help her plan and implement Intel's new CD-ROM, Data on Demand. This product would take those 16,600 pages and first put them on CD-ROM in the field sales offices of Intel to back up the printed documents. Eventually, Intel would sell the product to customers. Intel contracted with R.R. Donnelley, the world's largest private printer, to produce the disc. I would be on Intel's side in defining the disc and approving it.

Donnelley had been hanging around the CD-ROM world for years, trying to figure out where they fit. Some of its book publishing customers had produced CD-ROMs without them, and they, like Dialog years earlier, didn't want to miss out on the action. And if a CD-ROM didn't just supplement the printed work, but replaced it, then Donnelley felt especially threatened. Who could argue with replacing a printed work with a CD-ROM?—especially if it was a big bulky book that changed each month or year or was just thrown out. What about the estimated 30 percent of all documents that companies discarded because they overprinted? Then there were the reduced storage and shipping costs. There were many advantages of CD-ROM over books in the arena of technical documentation.

Courtesy Hewlett-Packard

*HP's LaserROM was the first product to place documents on CD-ROM and use CD-ROM to support customers. LaserROM contained the equivalent of a stack of books 25 feet high.*

Sheri's CD-ROM, as the name stated, was an "on-demand" product. That meant that users could print out what they needed on-demand, when they wanted it. With the CD-ROM, nothing was ever out of stock in the field offices, and finding documents was as easy as typing a word. The Intel product had a straightforward, definable purpose and was well-received. The bread and butter of CD-ROM—where it fit best—was always where there were several reasons for using it.

Sheri hopped on a plane when the product was finished and traveled around the world to Intel offices, training people on the new product. It became the standard way Intel distributed documents. Not only was it cheaper, but other benefits turned up, like being able to do a custom printout exactly to a customer's specifications, or finding things with a keyword search that were hidden among those thousands of pages.

Intel's contribution to "techdoc" was the on-demand aspect, because Sheri realized that CD-ROM was just a tool to get custom-delivered documents to people who needed them, when they needed them. Hewlett-Packard delivered monthly more than 500,000 pages of computer system documentation to customers after LaserROM arrived on the scene in 1988. They included manuals, application notes, software status bulletins, and other support information traditionally delivered on paper or answered over the phone. Following in HP's footsteps, soon Apple, DEC, IBM, National Semiconductor and Texas Instruments delivered their documents on CD-ROM.

CD-ROM and techdoc were natural companions. Who could argue with something that is smaller, cheaper, and faster? And since a CD-ROM could store the equivalent of several large trees worth of paper, who could argue with a technology that helped save trees?

# thirteen

## Guinness is Good for You
## 1990

GUINNESS PLC IS A MULTINATIONAL CONGLOMERATE THAT OWNS Guinness Publishing and Guinness Brewing, and is headquartered in London. Guinness Publishing publishes many fun and informational books, most notably the *Guinness Book of Records*. This book, and others, are considered "intellectual property" in the trade, and are licensed by third parties for publication on CD-ROM. Intellectual property is the raw material of CD-ROM.

Intellectual property is a creative work or expression of an idea. When you use a piece of software or read a book, you really don't own it, the owner of the intellectual property is giving you certain rights to use it. You can't just copy the book and resell it under a different name for example. Rich Bowers calls intellectual property a "license to steal." He says that what you are really doing is letting someone take something with them to use, letting them take it off the shelf and home, or essentially stealing it.

When you buy a piece of property to build a house, rules are associated with the transaction. Certain characteristics of the property make up its value, including the location, slope or grade of the land, compactness of the soil, proximity to flood zones, and availability of water and electricity—and its proximity to the nearest fault lines.

With intellectual property, you can't build houses on it, but you can make CD-ROMs out of it. Intellectual property can be just about anything related to information including books, magazines, photos, movies, poems, and information, and also patents. Intellectual property has characteristics like real property, and is judged on such things as its reputation, how popular is it, how current is it, what does it cover, how accurate is it and most important, is it unique and do people value the information? Will they pay money for it? These characteristics usually add up to a price that is paid to license the intellectual property, to do something else with it, like make a CD-ROM. Try to find those characteristics, or the rules and regulations of intellectual property as it applies to CD-ROM written down anywhere, and you'll have a hard time.

Owning valuable intellectual property can be exactly like owning a piece of downtown Manhattan—you just sit and wait for the highest bidder.

The *Guinness Book of Records* is the best-selling copyrighted book in the world. It has sold over 65 million copies. That's an unbelievable statistic for a book that started as a way to settle bets in British pubs.

Several weeks after I submitted my proposal to work on Guinness to Patrick Gibbins, I began to understand the situation better. Patrick was president of Pergamon Compact Solution (PCS), a sister company to the original company on which Robert Maxwell built his empire, Pergamon Press. Pergamon

Compact Solution was a favorite of Ian Maxwell, one of the Maxwell sons actively involved in running the business. PCS was licensing, with Maxwell's money, the *Guinness Book of Records* from another small but respectable company that was part of another British powerhouse.

PCS seemed to have everything going for it: a high-profile, dynamic company forging new ground with an exciting technology. Now they owned the CD-ROM rights to the *Guinness Book of Records* and were about to come out with the first product. They accepted my proposal, which was an honest attempt to explain how we could market a consumer-oriented CD-ROM when no distribution channels existed. We all agreed that we would use the Guinness disc to break down barriers to wider distribution of CD-ROM.

"Owning the rights" to a disc, as PCS did with Guinness, can mean lots of things. It's similar to having a friend say, "I own a piece of that company." Unless you know several things, ranging from the size of "that company" to the percentage ownership and options of the supposedly wealthy friend, you can't judge the value of what he holds. You can't judge the value of "owning the rights" to a CD-ROM product until you see the agreement and understand some non-contractual items like the market dynamics of CD-ROM.

Contracts covering these issues in CD-ROM may be as long as fifty pages. Since there are few rules in CD-ROM, many contractual elements have been borrowed from other industries, especially book publishing, software, and movie production. Then, too, some shorter agreements are derived entirely from the book of common sense.

We spent a hectic Fall 1989 promoting the product before its release on a Macintosh platform, and setting up U.S. distribution. Though it was small, we were getting advance orders for hundreds of units, which was promising. Then in February 1990, I had my first real lesson in the hardball intellectual property business, which could be known as dataopoly—in this particular game, Guinness was Park Place.

The day I expected our first shipment of Guinness CD-ROMs from PCS, I put in a call to London to see why they hadn't arrived. There was no answer. The next day there was no answer. Several days later, I got a call from Cally Brown, an energetic marketeer who had been a champion of this product. She was calling from home.

What Cally said shocked and saddened me: Robert Maxwell had closed down PCS lock, stock, and barrel. It no longer existed. Everyone at PCS was fired. After a quick chat with Cally, I thanked her for calling, got off the phone, and tried to decide what to do.

According to Cally, most of the PCS assets, including the Guinness project, were being transferred to a company named Mirrorsoft, which was a computer game company that Maxwell also owned. She also implied that Ian Maxwell, Robert's son, was the one who had formally closed down PCS. After getting no response from the Mirrorsoft people, I got angry and called London to get the number for Maxwell Communications.

"Is Ian Maxwell in?" I inquired, realizing I was a stranger asking for a man responsible for a multibillion dollar enterprise. After being transferred through several layers of administrative assistants, I reached someone who identified herself as Ian Maxwell's assistant, who told me he wasn't in.

"Please give him a message. I am going to fax him today and call in the morning," I told her. I then sent off a fax telling him that, among other things, his decision had put me in the uncomfortable situation of setting up distributors for a new product and not being able to deliver—not even being able to tell them a good reason why I couldn't deliver.

Much to my surprise, when I called the next day, I got right through to Ian and we had a short but pleasant conversation. He had already told the president of Mirrorsoft about me and said I should call him, which I did the following day. He let me know he wanted to continue the relationship, and the product would be delivered, but late.

The relationship with Mirrorsoft was in sharp contrast with PCS. Whereas, PCS had an enthusiasm for both the product and the relationship with me, Mirrorsoft seemed to look at both as leftover bits of the PCS carcass. The Guinness product had been the PCS flagship product, but at Mirrorsoft it lost out to a computer game version of Teenage Mutant Ninja Turtles. It was downright embarrassing and it wasn't even a close race, since that product sold better than all the consumer products for CD-ROM from all the companies in the world combined. The relationship continued but was strictly business. I was originally hired as a consultant to set up distributors and Mirrorsoft wanted me instead to act as the distributor, which I agreed to. The product started to do very well after the PC version of Guinness was released, and was included in many bundle packages with CD-ROM drives.

Britannica Software, which was transforming itself into Compton's NewMedia, put in an order for 1,000 discs, which was unheard of at the time. As a result, they quickly became "most favored dealer." Tom McGrew, vice president of marketing for Compton's NewMedia, decided that Guinness would be the first product they would sell with their popular Compton's Multimedia Encyclopedia. In a room behind the Compton's booth in Chicago at the Consumer Electronics Show, Tom explained they wanted to open up the consumer market through mass distribution. I explained

Courtesy Compton's NewMedia

*Norm Bastin, senior vice president and general manager (sitting) and Tom McGrew, vice president of marketing, built Compton's NewMedia into a CD-ROM powerhouse. Famous for their Compton's Multimedia Encyclopedia, they were the first major distributor for the Guinness Disc of Records, and later became the publisher.*

to him that we had a product for that purpose but didn't have the resources to distribute it. Our collaboration was a boon for the product and for my relationship with Mirrorsoft, though our numbers were way off the quarter million units of "The Turtles" that shipped. Now there were three established names associated with this product: Compton's (Britannica), Guinness, and Maxwell—UniDisc was somewhere in the middle doing a juggling act.

Another phone call came from London. A Mirrorsoft manager called to tell me they were breaking their contract with Guinness and backing out of the project. Again I was orphaned, less than a year after Maxwell closed down PCS.

Evidently, Guinness had not yet been informed. I called the only person who would understand my predicament—the former president of PCS, Patrick Gibbins. We had a good discussion and I asked him what to do. It became clear that I should contact Guinness directly, which I did the following day.

I called Donald McFarlan, editor of the *Guinness Book of Records*. I informed Donald that Mirrorsoft was going to break their contract, and that I wanted to continue since I was too far into this product to back out. I told him I had just shipped thousands of units of the disc, all of which listed my company's name on the manual for technical support. By breaking its agreement with me, Mirrorsoft had left my business in a position of having to answer hundreds of technical questions for no revenue.

After some discussion, it sounded like I had a comrade in Donald and we had a common enemy: Mirrorsoft. We began to discuss a direct relationship between Guinness and UniDisc. I was introduced to the only person in the world I knew who had the title of "Information Agent," Tony Feldman. He and I began picking up the pieces.

Tony Feldman sold information to the highest bidder and his revenue came from commissions on sales. For years I had tried to build the trust of book publishers, talking about win-win situations. Tony Feldman talked about the evils of CD-ROM companies like UniDisc who wanted to rip off book publishers by paying below market royalties. Needless to say, when I started talking about paying Guinness tens of thousands of dollars for publishing rights to this new, unstable, and emerging market, Tony came back with a counter offer close to ten times that for what he characterized as a "valuable commodity."

The money was getting out of my range, and I wanted to nail down the deal before it went out to Tony's open market. I decided to call in the "most favored dealer": Compton's NewMedia. After some negotiating on both ends, I got the amount Tony wanted to about equal the amount Compton's would guarantee, and we had a deal. On the Friday before 1990's Microsoft CD-ROM show, I signed the contract with Guinness in the morning. Several hours later, I had a distribution agreement with Compton's NewMedia to cover the royalties and development costs.

I had gone from Consultant to Distributor to Publisher in a year—Compton's had gone from Dealer to Distributor to

Exclusive Distributor—Guinness had had three different publishers. Robert Maxwell died a few months later, and I began studying the complicated web of his companies, trying to figure out where Mirrorsoft fit.

We hustled to produce our own version of the Guinness disc but didn't have much time. I hired Kim Woodward, a student at the University of California at Santa Cruz, as a technical support person. He quickly began managing the entire production process of a multimedia version of Guinness, complete with text, pictures, and sound. He scanned 300 35mm slides one-by-one, produced hundreds of picture captions, digitized the sounds, and linked everything together. Part of the deal with Compton's NewMedia was to use its software, so we delivered the information to them and they "Smartrieved" it, turning it into a multimedia CD-ROM. We also decided to try some new packaging called the Digipack to better display the product. We put the first version out in a world-record time of three months.

When the product was finished, I took a trip to London to meet the Guinness people and show the product to the press. I met Mark Cohen, president of Guinness Publishing, Donald McFarlan, and Tony Feldman. It was in the morning and McFarlan just finished speaking when he suddenly got up to leave.

"Let's go," he said, "otherwise we won't be able to talk." McFarlan and I headed out the back door, and I caught a glimpse of some people in the front reception area "Almost every day someone comes by," he explained to me, "to say they broke a world record. We have a form for them to fill out but they still want to come by." The reception area at Guinness Publishing couldn't hold more than a couple people. As editor, he was obviously a busy and wanted man, managing 7,000 world records and the people holding them.

My relationship with Guinness got better as time went on, and we talked about publishing other books on CD-ROM. I disliked, though, being caught between two companies like Guinness and Britannica and as they both made more demands on me, I decided to get out of the middle. We entered into a three-way agreement, effectively making Compton's the publisher, handling all the costs of the product, then paying me. It was also a better position for UniDisc. Compton's became the fourth publisher of the Guinness Disc in three years.

Soon I realized even more, I needed to get out of the middle and let Compton's and Guinness deal directly on issues, something they both expressed a desire to do. They began to discuss the contract renewal, but an interesting thing happened in the middle of their talks. The price of property went up...the intellectual property.

Microsoft was reportedly buying up rights and pushing up the price of selected rights, having just bought 26 percent of British publisher Dorling Kindersley, a $70 million company known for its highly illustrated, (i.e., "good for multimedia"), titles including such things as Your Baby and Child and The Family Medical Guide. Shortly after hearing this news, I received a call from Tony.

"We have had an offer for the Guinness rights that is substantially higher than what Compton's offered," he said. "Does Compton's want to increase its offer?"

By this time, I was tired of paying rent on a piece of property in downtown Manhattan and so was Compton's, and we thought it was only a bluff. We declined to raise the offer, and several weeks later I got a fax from Tony informing me that Guinness had signed an agreement with another CD-ROM publisher. We all speculated. Who was it? Microsoft? Sony? Maybe Grolier, a competitor of Compton's?

A few months later, the courtesy call came from the president of Grolier Electronic Publishing. They were the fifth publisher in three years.

In the early 1900s Guinness Brewing had a classic ad campaign for its beer that is forever etched in the minds of the people of England. "Guinness is good for you," was their tasteful motto.

Now it might be more appropriate to say that when it comes to CD-ROM, "The Guinness Book is good for Guinness."

# fourteen

## Keeping Up with the World's Fastest Talker
## 1991

LIONS, TIGERS AND BEARS. TEXT, PICTURES AND SOUND. LIONS, tigers and bears. One you yell when you're scared in the woods, and the other you chant when you're getting into multimedia, which can be just as scary.

Text, pictures and sound are the meat of multimedia. Of course, there are other things people always want to include on the list, like video and animation, but they're still just mixtures of the Big Three—text, pictures and sound. Video is fast-moving pictures with sound, and animation is moving, illustrated pictures and characters. Though we have five senses, the computer can only *show* us pictures and words, let us *hear* sounds, and let us *touch* the keyboard. It can't handle our senses of smell and taste.

When the responsibility of publishing the Guinness disc landed in our lap, we had little time to think. We knew we had to

*Steve Woodmore and Steve Briers, the world's fastest forward and backward talkers. They have been waging a battle to gain recognition in the U.S. as the rightful holders of their respective world records.*

take the three basic elements and combine them. First, there was the text, about 7,000 records. Then came the pictures, which included 300 photos in a variety of formats, including 35mm slides and prints. Finally was the sound which Guinness didn't have—we'd have to dream that up.

The sound was the most difficult. We quickly went through the book and highlighted records that would lend themselves to sound or music. There were the obvious ones including animal sounds, musical instruments, and famous speeches. These, though, could have been part of any electronic encyclopedia and weren't unique to Guinness. We planned a mix of those sounds with several others that characterized the uniqueness of Guinness: the World's Fastest Talker, the World's Fastest Backwards Talker, and we had an inkling that maybe we could do something with the Longest Words in several languages.

Through Guinness, I contacted the World's Fastest Talker and World's Fastest Backwards Talker. Steve Woodmore, the World's Fastest Talker, lives in London and is a computer salesman, and he was game to be on the disc. We then discussed a "talk-off" between him and John Moschitta, who many people in the United States think of as the fastest talker. This irked Steve, who went on to say that John Moschitta had tricked the people in the U.S. into thinking he was the fastest in the world.

"He doesn't even belong on the same stage with me. I've beaten him twice publicly now. He can't even do 600 words per minute." Then Steve did something I'd hear half a dozen times over the next several months, he said "listen" then proceeded to talk at an amazing clip. I was convinced, but I was no expert in fast talking.

Steve Briers was the World's Fastest Backwards Talker and also lived in the U.K. Not surprisingly, the Steves were friends, though an odd couple. Woodmore was brash and forward, Briers acted like someone who possessed a mystical talent that even he couldn't fully explain.

"Talking backwards is like speaking another language," he'd say. "It's something I started when I was young, and one of the first things I mastered was reading license plates backwards." Briers, too, had his American counterpart who got under his skin, David Fuhrer.

We came up with a script that both could follow. They'd introduce themselves, then give a mini-lesson on how to do their craft. Next, each would launch into the passage he used to break the world's record—in Woodmore's case a passage from Tom Clancy's *Patriot Games*, and for Brier it was the lyrics from the rock group Queen's "Night at the Opera." Coincidentally, at the time, both works were high profile in the U.S. The movie *Patriot Games* was coming out and the movie *Wayne's World* featured the Queen song.

I contacted the University of California Santa Cruz linguistics department, and spoke to a professor about the World's Longest Words. We devised a plan to record six people saying the longest words in their languages, and using them in sentences. He wanted to participate to make sure the project was done with linguistic integrity, and helped us recruit the people.

Sound on a computer, if it's done with style and imagination, is the most powerful experience a computer can deliver, especially when mixed with visuals. It goes straight to the emotions. There is no real separation with sound, as there is with pictures and words. Sound fills the room and you really don't care or notice exactly where it's coming from, which results in a feeling of immersion. With words and pictures, there is a tangible separate feeling from not being able to put your head inside a computer.

Several months later, I was demonstrating the software features and unique content of the Guinness Disc to a pretty serious trade show crowd in San Francisco. There was about five minutes to go in my thirty-minute speech. Kim was my assistant, "playing the keyboards" on the computer while I talked.

"Now we'll play you a sample of some sound that is on the disc," I said, planning for the sound to bring my talk to a close.

"Hi. My name is Steve Woodmore," a voice with a British accent proclaimed over the speakers hooked up to the CD-ROM, "and I hold the world record for being the World's Fastest Talker."

With each word that Woodmore spoke, another face lit up, until a loud group laugh broke out. Then I heard "Shhhh" from people who wanted to listen to him speak fast. It was a miraculous transformation of a crowd. We continued to play sounds from the disc, including the calls of an extinct bird, recorded in 1935 when the bird and his kind were still around, and a little music from the Grammy Awards, which we had licensed for use on the disc, because select Grammy Awards were listed in the Guinness book.

The reaction of the crowd had been relatively calm since the fast talkers until a voice that was stretching to speak the English language said, "The longest word in the Russian language is Ryentgyenoelyektrokardiografichyeskogo." Given the fact that the USSR as we knew it was being dismantled, it was no surprise that the whole room cracked up when he translated his sentence as "The X-ray electrocardiographic is no more." We left that conference room with an up feeling, along with our audience.

Stories of kids trying to keep up with the fastest talkers or recite the longest words filtered our way, and only confirmed the power of sound. The text and pictures of the Guinness disc were fun, too, and they provoked an endless stream of questions.

We took many photos of the product, and featured certain ones as the product signature to be repeated in ads and promotions. The cheetah, which is the Fastest Land Mammal, was used because there was a good picture of a cheetah in the book, showing it as it raced across the open plains of East Africa. We used the cheetah to accompany speeches, and once I loaned the picture to someone who had to give a speech on CD-ROM.

"Have you looked closely at that cheetah picture?" Steve Shaffer called after giving his talk. I didn't know what he was talking about. He said "Read it carefully, especially what's written about the cheetah. Call me back after you've pulled your hair out."

So I sat down to read it. It all looked fine—and then it hit me like a ton of bricks.

"...the cheetah runs apartment out at 65 mph..."

Apartment out. Apartment out. What did it mean? Oh no, I thought, our British-to-American translation was done by hand. We read over everything, how did this one slip in?

I called Steve back. He was already slightly uneasy about CD-ROM quality control because he had purchased the rights to a series of volumes called the *Particle Atlas*, used in identifying particles under a microscope. In a police department or laboratory, it was critical that the information was correct, so we had many talks about quality control and CD-ROM. He understood that keeping all the data correct in translating the *Particle Atlas* to CD-ROM would be a chore.

Steve described his talk, "Someone in the audience noticed it and wanted to know if they could have the slide as an example of the inadequacies of automated translation. At first I thought it was just a typo, but he figured out that a British 'flat' was an American 'apartment,' so if a cheetah runs 'flat out' at 65mph, it would be translated to 'apartment out.'"

"Please send me that slide," I said. "I'm going to destroy all of them personally."

Everyone was moving quickly into multimedia, which was supposed to be a complex task. But for us, it wasn't the pictures or sounds that got us. It was the words.

# fifteen

## The CD-ROM Name Game 1992

*It is written that the CD begat CD-ROM which begat CD-I. And then the sky opened up and multimedia appeared, in all its splendor. The people rejoiced, for finally they understood. The children learned, the trees grew, and the couch potatoes played with their clickers—their interactive clickers.*

*And then the CD-ROM gods said to the CD-ROMers, "You must play the CD-ROM Name Game. You must make up letters. You must then build a new technology around these letters. Do not worry if the people do not understand."*

*"People will become confused and wonder whether CD-I is really a part of the almighty CD-ROM family, or if it is the beginning of something new." Megagod, god of mass storage said, "Do not worry, it will work out."*

The tremendous success of the CD in the music industry provided a firm foundation for CD-ROM. The standard for CD audio, developed by Sony and Philips was known as the "Red Book" standard (for the color of the document cover). The Red Book standard provided a way for "16-bit, 44.1 Kilohertz" sound to be played on all manufacturers' CD players. The clear sound that comes out of a CD player is digital sound that is sampled 44.1 times per second. Each time a snapshot, or sample, is taken, 16 pieces of information are recorded about that sound. The audio CD also provided limited ability to store graphics on a CD, but was never successfully implemented.

Based on the Red Book standard, a new standard for CD-ROM called the Yellow Book, or ISO 9660, was adopted with the help of several companies who had a lot to gain from standardizing the industry. It provided a standard for data (such as text, graphics, photos, etc.) to be put on a CD and accessed using a computer. It gave CD-ROM the level of standardization needed to put products into the marketplace. A "mixed mode" disc was one that placed audio and data on one disc, with the data taking the first track, and audio having several options for being stored on successive tracks.

The High Sierra Group, named for its first meeting at the High Sierra Hotel at Lake Tahoe, was a loosely-knit group of people who had written the first CD-ROM standard, which eventually turned into the Yellow Book standard. The lack of communication about compatibility of hardware and software caused quite a bit of confusion in the early days of the industry.

Not only did the music industry give CD-ROM the basis for its new standard, it also gave CD-ROM the mastering facilities to make the discs. The early pricing for making discs were the same prices as for CD audio discs, just printed on the CD-ROM price sheet. With many early CD-ROM developers wanting to

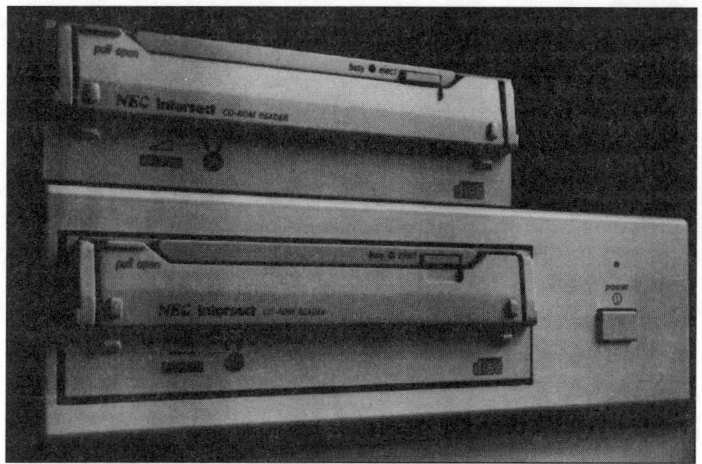


*A CD-ROM drive looks similar to a CD player for music, except it usually has no front panel controls (like play, pause, etc.) and hooks up to a computer.*

print only 25 or 50 discs to get a product into the market, pricing at that low production level could be prohibitive—as high as $10,000 per master, plus $25 per disc.

With CD-ROM, the compact disc suddenly became a tremendously rich environment, capable of storing the highest quality audio, along with dazzling color pictures, text, graphics, and animation. When the computer controlled the CD-ROM drive, any spot on the disc was instantly accessible, allowing pictures, sound, and text to be mixed and presented in new ways, and giving the user a new level of involvement. Applications for this technology were not difficult to imagine: books that talked, movies that interacted with viewers, programs that were self-teaching. An added bonus was a built-in 16-bit Digital Audio Converter (DAC) on the CD-ROM drive, instantly equipping the computer with sound. A host of new words were coined to represent this phenomenon, including

Infotainment, Edutainment, New Media (which has caught on in Japan) and most recently, Interactive Multimedia.

The reason for the initial success of CD-ROM was the most practical, and to many people, the most boring aspect of the technology. That was its ability to store and access amazing amounts of text—about 250,000 pages fit on a single disc. Thousands of color pictures could be put on a single disc. But with CD-quality audio, the space on the disc suddenly looked pretty small, with a maximum of 72 minutes available for play—not much if you planned to add background music, narration, or speeches. The text, pictures, and audio all had to share a disc, which could cause severe space limitations.

There had to be a way to store more audio on a disc. CD-ROM XA, an enhancement to the Yellow Book standard, added the capability of storing different frequencies and sampling rates for audio—an option for storing compressed 4-bit audio at 18.9KHz or 37.8KHz. CD-ROM XA proponents touted "16 hours of audio" on a CD-ROM. This was true at the lower sampling rates that were suitable primarily for simple speech, voice-over or sound effects. Also, CD-ROM XA provided for interleaving of files, so that a picture and sound could be stored together. More importantly, this meant they could be taken off the disc and played together. Since this capability involved compression, it also required a new piece of hardware to decompress the audio. Unfortunately, most CD-ROM drives today do not have that ability.

Seeing the need for a consumer CD-based technology, still another standard was introduced, the Green Book standard. Green Book was the first standard to link a CD-ROM drive directly to a television set, and added another audio option to CD-ROM, 8-bit at 37.8KHz. Philips introduced the trade name for this technology, CD-I, in 1986, and began shipping the first drives and discs in 1991, reportedly spending $500 mil-

Photo courtesy of Philips

*CD-I reached the market in 1992 to try and capture the "CD-ROM in the home" market, by hooking directly to a television set, without requiring a computer. The unit looks just like a CD music player.*

lion getting it out the door. Philips projects 12 million CD-I players in households by 1997, and is using its 25,000 retail outlets to get CD-I into the marketplace.

Commodore, meanwhile, decided to move quickly and shipped CDTV as a direct competitor to CD-I for the consumer, announcing the product in 1990 and shipping in 1991. With a target market of homes and schools, Commodore projected initial shipments of 150,000 to 400,000 units the first year. It made a point of not mentioning the word "computer" in promotions, though many knew that inside the slightly-larger-than-usual CD player was a little Amiga computer. Commodore also avoided the question of whether it competed with CD-I, saying the products were for "different applications." However, the discs that accompanied each technology were strikingly similar: consumer products, fun things, and games.

Commodore had a master spokesperson for its CDTV introduction at the Consumer Electronics Show in Chicago in the summer of 1991. Nolan Bushnell, who over a decade earlier had transformed a bar game named Pong into a huge company named Atari, spoke about CDTV being the next big thing in consumer entertainment. The CDTV version of the Guinness Disc of Records was one of the featured discs. Jim Mackonochie, who had also been the chairman of the board of several Maxwell companies, including Pergamon Compact Solution, was at the press conference. He had become one of the key people behind CDTV since Maxwell had closed down his companies, and sent him packing.

Next, Kodak then entered the interactive multimedia race using the only element so far not exploited in CD-ROM: pictures. With Kodak's 1992 introduction of Photo CD, your local Fotomat (for less than $20, including prints) can take the film from your camera and turn it into, you guessed it, CD-ROM discs. These discs can be taken home and viewed on a television set, using a Kodak Photo CD player. The discs can also be "bridge" discs, viewed and edited on a computer, too. Photo CD was introduced in 1992, and new features planned include the ability to add text and sound to the pictures, all based on the CD-ROM XA standard.

CD-I, CDTV, and Photo CD have several things in common. First, the main goal is to show the products on a television set, with a simple device similar to a TV remote control. All are moving into uncharted waters by bringing interactive multimedia into the home. The initial reaction of the market to CD-I and CDTV has been lukewarm, with fewer than 10,000 units of each shipping in the U.S in the first year. When people are used to the slick quality of television and the speed and action of video games, the CD-based products look sluggish. Digital images may look a bit grainy, and while a CD-ROM drive has many assets, one of its weaknesses is that it is slow to retrieve the information from the disc. It's a big move from sound to text, but a giant leap to multimedia extravaganzas.

Tandy introduced its VIS (Video Information System) in 1992, to provide a "fun, informative learning experience for the whole family any time you want it." Tandy did a good job of analyzing the other home CD-ROM technologies. It tried to provide better technology and more incentive for publishers to make VIS discs. However, since people could purchase a "home computer" from Tandy for not much more than the price of the entertainment system, the VIS failed to attract many buyers.

Things change, though, as CD-ROM drives speed up, and technologies add new features. The ability to interchange discs (play CD-I discs on a Photo CD player) is another promise of most manufacturers. Probably the biggest phenomenon tying the major companies together is the age-old concept of "betting the bank." Over a billion dollars was spent to develop CD-I, CDTV, Photo CD, and VIS technologies, and each company has prominently positioned its entrant as a critical, long-term strategic move for the company. Seeing CD-ROM affecting the bottom line of a large company indicates the level of expectation for the technology.

What about the CD-ROM drives hooked to personal computers instead of televisions? Intel was busy during the late '80s acquiring another emerging technology from GE, named DV-I for Digital Video Interactive. The developers of DV-I made CD-ROM capable of full screen, full-motion video. Without DV-I, the 30 frames per second for video require so much storage that less than a minute could fit on a CD-ROM. DV-I is based on the Yellow Book CD-ROM standard, but requires additional hardware from Intel. Most applications are in the corporate training area.

There are other problems associated with turning computers with CD-ROM drives into multimedia maestros. Anyone who has a computer on his desk knows the frustration of incompatibilities that get in the way of solving problems. With much fanfare, the Software Publishers Association announced the Multimedia Personal Computer (MPC) in 1991—a hardware and software platform for multimedia. MPC supports many audio options, as well as a subset of the MIDI (Musical Instrument Digital Interface), or synthesizer, specification. The MPC specification includes a built-in sound board on the computer, equivalent to a low-end synthesizer. MPC also includes an on-board sound digitizer, giving people the ability to record and edit their own sound. MPC computers can be purchased as fully-packaged units, or as upgrades to existing PCs.

Where has Apple been while all this has been going on? Most CD-ROM developers agree that the Macintosh is still the easiest computer used for development. Apple had the forethought to build an 8-bit DAC into the computer, putting sound on all Macintosh users' desks. While only about 20 percent of the available CD-ROMs are for the Macintosh, that group includes the most discs with sound. Apple developed QuickTime, which will allow Macintoshes to play video in a small screen in a window. QuickTime movies will eventually be transportable across most computers. This means a QuickTime movie can be developed on the Macintosh, put on a CD-ROM, and used on an IBM PC or Photo CD player. Microsoft quickly responded to QuickTime with Video for Windows, a product with similar capabilities for producing and displaying video under Microsoft Windows.

In Japan, in 1990, when Sony began shipping its CD-ROM version of the Sony Walkman, the Data Discman, it had no idea that 70,000 units would sell within three months. These small units play 3" mini-CD discs, have a pop-up screen about 3.5" wide, and weigh less than two pounds. Forget hooking CD-ROM up to a TV set or a computer—the Data Discman is totally self-contained. In 1991, the units shipped in the U.S., and while they attained nowhere near their popularity in Japan, they are being used as portable information devices by many people who need to travel and take information with them.

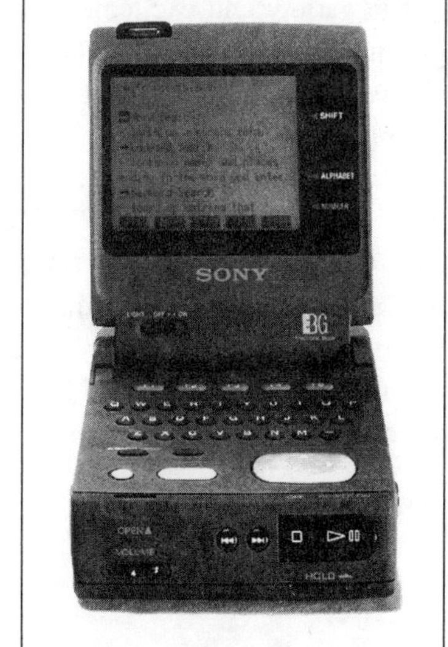


Courtesy Sony Corporation

*The Data Discman fits in the palm of your hand and can hold hundreds of thousands of pages of information, besides playing audio and showing pictures.*

The Sony MiniDisc entered the market in 1992, looking like a replacement for the cassette, now 30 years old and looking like it might go the way of the LP record album. This 2.25" disc, and portable player, can both play and record. There are no CD-ROM products built for it, but the possibility of low-cost, portable recorders generates excitement in the CD-ROM community.

The generically named "Sony Portable CD-ROM XA Player" followed in 1992, called the Bookman within the industry. Now called MMCD or Multimedia CD, it is slightly larger but still self-contained and plays standard CD-ROM discs. It also contains, like the Data Discman, a little keyboard that is exposed when the screen pops up. The keys on the keyboard are small, but well-designed. The weekly full-page ads in *Newsweek*, showing an elegant MMCD next to a Bird of Paradise, are an indication of the financial commitment Sony has to this device.

The variety and excitement generated by these new technologies have caused many to call this period a Renaissance of sorts, where creative energies abound. Then, too, there are a lot of people who are just plain confused, and wondering "who's making the decisions up there." The only technology today with a history is the standard CD-ROM, mostly used on DOS or Macintosh computers. Whether you are a user or a developer, that's where the greatest number and variety of products and buyers are to be found. However, that scene could change quickly as the marketing muscle of Philips, Sony, and others bring their vision of the future into people's homes, schools, and offices.

# sixteen

## Beating Microsoft at Multimedia Hardball 1992

ABOUT A MONTH BEFORE THE ANNUAL "MICROSOFT SHOW" (now called Intermedia), someone called from Microsoft asking permission to use the information from the *Guinness Book of Records* for a product demonstration at the upcoming show. Guinness had told her to contact me. At the time, we had been publishing the Guinness disc for several months, and Microsoft showed the usual curious surprise when they learned that a small company owned the rights to this popular book.

I told her that I probably would not allow its use because it might jeopardize our relationship with Compton's NewMedia, and we left it at that. She didn't say anything more about the intended use because she said it was confidential.

The Microsoft show, as it was known in the industry, had undergone many changes since its inception in 1986 as the "First International Conference on CD-ROM." With 1,100 attendees

*Sony, Microsoft, and Compton's NewMedia all introduced MMCD software in 1992. Microsoft hoped to publish the Guinness disc on an MMCD, pictured here.*

and 100 people from the press, and for $1000 registration fee, the show was clearly not for your average guy with a CD-ROM drive. At the first show, people from the industry proudly reported that 11,300 CD-ROM drives had been shipped worldwide, 420 masters had been manufactured (most of them demos or test discs), and more than 28,000 copies of discs had been made. Since then, the conference had assumed a formidable role in the industry, especially because so many press people attended and the food was so good. Several name changes reflected the changing industry and changes in sponsorship.

Several days before the 1992 conference was to begin, another call came in from Microsoft. This time they faxed a non-disclosure form, which I signed. My phone contact went into some detail, and said Microsoft had built a prototype of a Guinness disc for a new product based on the Sony Bookman (eventually called Multimedia CD, or MMCD). I again said thanks, but no. I sent them a letter demanding that they destroy the disc and all the Guinness information, since both Guinness and I agreed that Microsoft had stepped over their bounds and were in violation of copyright law. The letter ended by saying that, "We must have your written assurance by the end of today that you will comply with the above." I also called and left the woman a voice mail message, requesting that they not show the prototype—otherwise, I would be forced to have someone stand around their booth to make sure they didn't do it. I didn't hear anything. It was March 6, and the show started March 10.

The day before the conference I got an urgent message from Microsoft at a San Francisco phone number. I called the number and the same woman answered the phone.

"Can you drive up here?" she asked. "We really need to work something out." I was over an hour away and didn't like the idea of driving up late at night, but I reluctantly said yes. She told me she was in a small room in the back of the Moscone Center.

I found the room and walked in, only to have 15 pairs of eyes focus nervously on me. They were all at tables with computers, shaped in a big square "U." I was in the middle of the "U." "Can we help you?" several of them said at once. I wasn't sure which one to answer.

"I'm here about Guinness," I said. Suddenly their faces changed from really uptight to only a little uptight. They knew who I was. "You must be Chris," a serious blonde woman said as she walked toward me, her hand extended.

She sat me down at a table and showed one of the most remarkable demonstrations of technology I have seen in a long time. It was the much-secretive Bookman, and it had a great demonstration of the Guinness product on it. Nice graphics, clever screens, and easy to use. It all fit nicely in a pair of cupped hands.

"Isn't that a great demo?" the woman's boss said, sitting next to one of the ten people watching my reaction. "We're going to be everywhere tomorrow—the *Wall Street Journal*, *Business Week*. It's the biggest thing at this show. Gates is going to talk about it." I could hear the forklifts in the room below moving boxes, setting up the last booths for the show. It was 9:00 p.m.

"It really looks nice," I said, "and that's exactly why you can't show it. I'm sorry, but you know that Compton's would kill me if I let you do this. You developed this demo with no permission to do so, and you must've known this was a risk. I'm going to have to ask you to destroy the disc, too, because you've ignored everything I've said so far. I understand you're in a jam, but I can't help that."

They explained that they had built two demos for the Bookman, and that's all they had to show. They showed me the other demo, a travel guide, which was far below the quality of Guinness. It looked like it had been slapped together, and wasn't really suitable for showing.

We talked for the better part of a couple hours, facing many painful silences while they tried to figure out how to convince me. Finally, Christine Doerr, the boss of the woman I had spoken with, conceded their blunder, and told me they were sorry. I could see by the defeated expression of the others that they thought I was a jerk, and the woman in charge was showing me why she was in charge. She was the only one in that room who would talk to me once we had decided that they wouldn't show it, and I respected her for her ability to rise above their failure.

"We have another problem," she said. "Both demos are on the same disc, so if we destroy the disc, we have absolutely nothing to show."

They had put both demos on one disc, with a fork at the beginning taking users to one or the other. After more discussion, we agreed to type letters of agreement in the room right that moment and sign them. The letter from Christine Doerr read as follows:

*"This letter confirms our discussion regarding the use of the Guinness data on our demo disc during the International Conference on Multimedia and CD-ROM. Microsoft agrees not to show the sample screens we've prepared using this*

*The Intermedia show, a.k.a. the Microsoft CD-ROM show, has become an annual meeting of CD-ROM (and multimedia!) industry veterans.*

*data, either on the show floor or in any other context. We apologize for the misunderstanding that resulted in having copyrighted material on the disc."*

It was signed and dated March 9, 1992. The show started in exactly ten hours. I signed it and typed out the letter to her, having a little trouble using Microsoft Word on a PC because I was used to writing on a Macintosh. It said:

*This letter confirms our conversation regarding Microsoft not showing the Guinness data from the CD-ROM disc. We understand that the Guinness data and your other demo are on the same disc, and we don't require that you destroy the disc. We do require that you do not allow anyone to go into the button entitled "Amazing Facts." UniDisc is exclusively licensed by Guinness to produce CD-ROM versions of the Guinness Book of Records."*

In a last-ditch attempt to convince me to let them show it, they had taken out all mention of Guinness, and called the demo "Amazing Facts." That, I explained to them, was no less a violation of copyright, but they still didn't seem to understand why I didn't want "free publicity" as they put it.

I signed the letter, shook her hand, and left. With the driving back and forth, I had only a few hours time to sleep before getting to the show on time. I couldn't resist visiting the Microsoft booth to spy. I saw a large crowd gathered around a small device showing travel information. Over at the Sony booth, I saw the same thing. The next morning, I read an article in the *Wall Street Journal* with the headline, "Microsoft, Sony To Pool Talents For New Device." It went on to say that the product, code-named the Bookman, was "part of an ambitious plan to create a hit product on par with Sony's Walkman...Microsoft said it will supply software tools and electronic titles." It didn't say that Microsoft had forcibly tried to become the sixth publisher of the Guinness Disc of Records.

As in other years, the conference showcased the changes in the industry, with more large companies exhibiting and fewer small ones. The Kodak, Pioneer, Sony, and Microsoft booths dwarfed those of smaller companies scattered around the edges. The price of booth space was twice as high as at a normal trade show. Likewise, the cost for registration remained high, attracting a select group of people who took CD-ROM seriously.

One big announcement was the merging of two leaders in the industry, Dataware Technologies and Reference Technology. Dataware was a German company run in the U.S. by David Wilcox. Dataware was a rising star in the industry, selling CD-ROM authoring software to more CD-ROM publishers than anyone else, by a long shot. Reference Technology was an early pioneer of CD-ROM. It was based in Colorado, and had apparently spent close to $30 million in venture capital since it was founded in the early '80s. Though Wilcox was careful to characterize the event as a merger, most people in the industry assumed it was an acquisition of Reference by Dataware. It was symbolic, watching one of the original CD-ROM companies running out of steam, seeing one of the new generation of companies coming in to take over.

In 1992, Microsoft was all over the newspapers and magazines. Bill Gates' stock rose and he was the richest man in the United States at the age of 37. Microsoft came out with its own electronic encyclopedia on CD-ROM, in direct competition with Compton's Multimedia Encyclopedia. Accusations of unfair trade practices were levied by the U.S. government against Microsoft, causing many small companies to come out of the woodwork with stories supporting the government's claims. A company that was once looked upon as an innovator began taking on the appearance of the neighborhood bully who had claimed his territory and it included everything: the sidewalks, the front yards, and the streets.

But I beat the bully. I had in inkling that this small victory was representative of struggles other small companies have had with Microsoft as it dominated an industry that was made up of small guys with big ideas. A few people who heard this story suggested I contact the government group investigating Microsoft, but I was satisfied with the score: Andrews – 1, Microsoft – 0.

# seventeen

## And the Grammy Goes to...
## 1992

EVERYONE IN THE CD-ROM INDUSTRY SECRETLY WISHES THEY made a living in Hollywood. Something magical happens when you go from making products that sell on floppy disks, known as software, to making products that sell on compact discs, and sell them as CD-ROMs. Music, pictures, and animation enter your life, and you want more...and more.

Making a CD-ROM about the Grammy Awards started as a kernel of an idea, a vague idea, that I stumbled upon accidentally. Originally, we obtained some sound and pictures from the Grammy Awards show to include on the Guinness CD-ROM. Later, the idea of combining information about past shows with pictures and sounds began to emerge as a real winner of a product. It had all the right elements: wide appeal across a range of ages, unique sound ("And the nominees are"...followed by short clips of nominated songs), and photos, and one of the most recognized names in the world—the Grammy Awards.

I took a trip to Burbank and met with Rob Senn, executive vice president and general manager of the National Academy of Recording Arts and Sciences, Inc. (NARAS). NARAS owned the Grammy Awards. He showed me around. In the back room was a very nice lady who was polite, but a little reluctant to explain what she was doing. Next to her were several file cabinets filled with index cards. Rob opened the files, and showed me tens of thousands of index cards, each one detailing a Grammy nominee or winner. They were old, dating back to 1958, and had obviously been handled a lot. The woman, it turned out, had spent the last couple years organizing the index cards, and inputting them into a computer—one by one. I wasn't surprised that she was protective about her database. It was the result of her work, and I wanted to take it away and put it on a CD-ROM. Next, Rob showed me the picture collection, and the videos from which we'd take the sound. In a few days, we signed an agreement, and were off and running.

I got to know Rob quickly. His responsibility was overwhelming—overseeing a show that featured the best musicians and was watched by over two billion people. Making a CD-ROM seemed trivial compared to that. Rob wanted to be actively involved in the product and see its progress, in contrast to many publishers with whom I worked. Usually they only wanted to see the finished product before it went out the door, and to make sure I kept up the royalty payments. However, Rob had some background in videodiscs, which allowed us to understand each other quickly through comparisons between videodiscs and CD-ROM.

I approached Compton's NewMedia about funding when I realized the project would require a large-scale marketing and promotion budget. Norm Bastin, president of Compton's NewMedia, and Tom McGrew, vice president of marketing, and I met in Las Vegas during Comdex to discuss the Grammy project. I realized the power of the Grammy association when we made a deal in less than half an hour. From my point of view, I was looking for a company to help fund the development and handle distribution. From their point of view, I was "delivering the Grammys," which commanded their attention. That week, Compton's announced the product at a press conference at the Hard Rock Cafe.

Martin Laracy, a top-notch engineer at Compton's, and I were assigned a spot backstage at the upcoming Grammy Awards to display a conceptual prototype we quickly put together. Besides showing the CD-ROM, we also put together an audio disc promoting the CD-ROM which was given to everyone attending the awards.

The audio disc was originally intended as a press release for the 200 press people at the show, but we decided to give it to everyone, all 5,000 attendees. We had so little time to make the disc that we had to make special arrangements with two companies, Disc Manufacturing, Inc. (DMI) to make the disc, and Golden Rule Printing to print the booklets. Pam Sansbury, a well-known, well-liked sales manager at DMI, pulled out all stops to get us a disc by Grammy night. The artwork went to the booklet printer on Monday, DMI got the booklets and our tape that Wednesday, and on Friday 5,000 finished discs were Federal Expressed from Huntsville, Alabama to New York City. DMI had turned around 5,000 discs in two days.

In the weeks leading up to the show, which was held in February 1992 at Radio City Music Hall in New York, I learned exactly what it meant to attend the Grammy Awards—not to mention that we were being allowed in an exclusive area only open to the press.

My travel agent asked me what I'd be doing in New York City. "I'm going to the Grammy Awards," I replied. "Well, excu-u-u-u-u-use me!" she shot back. In other words, being associated with the Grammy Awards gave me some kind celebrity status among my friends and associates. I must be someone if I was going there. I learned from Rob that there's such an incredible demand for tickets that even famous people will literally beg for them.

I checked into the Hyatt in New York City, picked up my press credentials, and walked over to Radio City Music Hall. I had a bright red day pass, allowing me to go in and set up the day before the show. The first thing I noticed as I approached the door were the people—lots of people standing outside the door. As I walked through the barriers, showing my badge, I realized who they were. They were the fans. For the next couple days, the world was divided into two groups of people: the fans and the celebrities. I decided that I belonged in some unidentifiable group, neither celebrity or fan, and promised myself I would never become a fan. A few minutes later, this turned out to be too much to ask.

I walked into the hallway and immediately realized that this was no ordinary demo set up. L.L. Cool J was up on stage blasting "Mama gonna knock you out," while a small group of people were milling around, talking and socializing. Looking at the faces, I realized that just about everyone was a celebrity. Not only were they celebrities, there was nothing separating them from me, we were all part of this same pre-show warm-up.

As I studied the room, the faces from television started to emerge. There was Bonnie Raitt, and Michael McDonald, and Paul Simon. I sat down for a few minutes to listen to the music, and said hi to the person sitting near me, and realized it was Luther Vandross. It was like being part of their world—they were relaxed and in their element—and they actually would talk to me.

Courtesy National Academy of Recording Arts and Sciences, Inc.

*The Grammy Award, the symbol of creative and technical excellence in the music industry, was first awarded in 1958.*

Martin and I set the prototype up in a small part of the press area, and spent the rest of the day listening to rehearsals. Martin had brought a little Instamatic camera, which was strictly against the rules, and would occasionally snap a quick picture. I found myself policing him, but at the same time knew that if it had been just me there I would never have taken such a risk. So, we developed an understanding, My role was to occasionally tell Martin not to do that, he would say "Okay," and then ignore me. He was obviously excited, and I just hoped he wouldn't become a full-fledged fan.

The next day, the day of the Grammys, we tested our prototype in the afternoon, put on our tuxedos, and were ready for action. The awards began, and after the celebrities made their way on stage to present or accept their awards, their next stop was the press room. We were positioned, by accident, where most celebrities waited before being interviewed by the press. There we were, among the celebrities and the press, showing a

CD-ROM. It was not an ordinary "Sir, would you like a demonstration," type of scene.

The night was a steady blur of celebrities—Roy Rogers, Ringo Starr, Natalie Cole, Willie Nelson, James Brown, and some younger hot groups like Boyz II Men and Color Me Badd. It's difficult to know what to say to someone who has just won a Grammy Award. It's difficult not to feel like a complete nerd among the hippest people in the world. I will always be thankful to B.B. King, who treated me "like I was someone," and talked for a few minutes. After that, saying, "Hi, how ya doin'?" to anyone who came past seemed no more difficult than circulating around a Christmas cocktail party.

Near the end of the awards, the press room suddenly got quiet, and I heard someone say, "She's coming." I turned around, and not more than five feet away was a grinning Barbra Streisand. "Hi, Barbra," I heard. "Hi, Barbra," I heard again. The room felt different, as though someone had turned down the music. Barbra Streisand was a special breed. She was no ordinary celebrity, she was a celebrity's celebrity.

A couple of the celebrities were quite interested in our CD-ROM, but we were competing with, and losing to, the real event of the evening—the show itself and the celebrities. The press people were interested in "doing a search" on the CD-ROM when they realized what we had on it. For example, when Natalie Cole won an award for her record made up of her father's songs, the *Hollywood Reporter* writers wanted to do a comparison of awards won by Nat King Cole and Natalie Cole. And, when a tie occurred, a dozen or so people from television, radio, and print learned that the last Grammy tie was in 1986 for Best Polka Recording by peering over our shoulders while Martin typed in "tie" and "sort by year."

Kurt Loder of MTV understood immediately not only what we were doing there, but why. He asked all the "right" questions—what was on the disc, when would it be available, and who was the target market?

The days following the Grammy show were a letdown, and for awhile everything seemed plain and boring. Martin developed his pictures and sent them to me, but they were disappointing because the camera did not capture what I felt. It was almost a religious event—seeing all the high priests and priestesses of music. Capturing that on film is like trying to take a picture of the inside of a church.

Bringing CD-ROM to the music business evolved as one of my personal goals after the Grammys. I realized that the real potential for quality CD-ROM production didn't lie in Silicon Valley, but instead, with the creative people who live and breathe music and pictures. The excitement generated around great music and the people who made that music was far beyond anything I will ever see at a computer trade show. The more I talked to people in the music business, the more I saw a desire on their part to learn about CD-ROM. Then, late in 1992, Paramount opened an office in Palo Alto, the heart of Silicon Valley. Apparently, I wasn't the only one thinking of combining Hollywood and Silicon valley.

Rob Senn became a comrade, someone who seemed to understand what I was trying to do. I wrote him several times asking, "Do you want Microsoft, the makers of MS-DOS, to be the company making the decisions about an exciting new entertainment medium?" Microsoft has always been the most powerful influence in CD-ROM, and as CD-ROM moved into entertainment and multimedia, that seemed like a crime.

In the '90s we will see a struggle for control of CD-ROM: a hybrid technology that combines elements of entertainment, publishing, and computers. Maybe someday there will be a Grammy Award for "Best Use of Sound in a Computerized Environment." Then we'll know that CD-ROM has really arrived.

# eighteen

## A TV Show Becomes Multimedia

## 1992

THE GRAMMY AWARDS ARE BESTOWED BY A GROUP OF accomplished music industry professionals who have gained entrance into the "Recording Academy." Academy members include singers, songwriters, engineers, and producers, as well some lesser-known people who write the liner notes on the insides of the packaging. The "Rule of 6" says that you can gain entrance into the Recording Academy once you have had at least six commercial nationwide releases. Grammy nominees are voted on by this group of people, and creative or technical excellence (as opposed to commercial success) is the main criteria for winning a Grammy.

As we began to develop the Grammy CD-ROM, it became clear that we had a standard to measure up to. We had to make a CD-ROM that matched the "creative excellence" of the Grammy Awards. Since the Grammy Awards are also about music, the

CD-ROM had to be about music. That meant not just having a database of musicians, or pictures of celebrities, but the sound and music itself on the Grammy disc had to be high quality and a feature of the product rather than an afterthought.

This challenge is not to be underestimated. It takes tremendous effort to turn a CD-ROM that can store loads of data and pictures into a musical medium. It is ironic, considering its origins that the strength of CD-ROM is not music—primarily because it takes so much room to store high-quality CD music. There is a direct relationship between quantity and quality: for some ideas to work, you need sufficient storage to hold enough music or pictures.

After putting the data and the pictures on the Grammy disc, we figured we had about 55 minutes left for music. That meant we had about a minute and a half for each year of the Grammy's 34 years. Somehow we had to condense 100 hours of videotape from these 34 years into 55 minutes that said it all.

On top of that, since the Grammy show on television is entertainment at its best, we had to make our CD-ROM entertaining. This, too, was a tremendous challenge. It's one thing to make a CD-ROM entertaining to the early adopters of technology and people in the computer industry. It's another to make something entertaining to people who know nothing about CD-ROM technology and expect the same quality they see on television or at the movies.

It is also difficult to take something that is already exciting and make it more so. The term "shovelware" was been cropping up in the CD-ROM industry to describe the plethora of boring, repetitive titles that were on the market. It was our goal to distance ourselves from those products. We wanted something unique, fun, and exciting. It was obvious that it would take more than intense audio editing to do the job.

The first step was to select the awards to feature and edit them down to a level that would present a good picture of the entire show. We produced highlights of each year and found it worked well to have short segments because it was music. Music communicates in a way that pictures or data, or even narration or sound effects can't. Music, especially if someone has heard it and liked it, has a powerful effect. Therefore, the impact, or "return on time," for the music far exceeded our expectations.

The next job was to synchronize the music with the pictures—not an easy chore with CD-ROM. On a CD-ROM, the pictures and the sound are two different types of data, stored in two different places on the disc. And if you want some text to appear on the screen with the picture, such as a caption for a photograph, then it is usually stored in a separate file somewhere else. How then do you time these three elements to work together when they aren't stored together?

What many people don't realize is that a CD-ROM drive automatically equips a computer with sound that can come directly out of the CD-ROM drive. Sound can come out of speakers or headphones plugged into the CD-ROM drive and other items that have to be synchronized with the sound appear on the monitor of the computer. The advantage to a sound board is that it can store more sound at lower quality levels, giving the CD-ROM publisher more options. But a sound board is an additional piece of hardware that not everyone has.

If you want to play a little music and show a picture then the process is fairly simple. But what if your pictures and text can't keep up with the speed of the music clips? I asked Tim Tully, who did the audio editing, to cut the sound as tightly as possible. Then we found that we almost went too far, and made the music move too quickly for the pictures to keep up. What if it's a long slide-show, and the amount of data you can get off the CD-ROM drive (i.e., the number of pictures) is too small to produce the entire show? What if the words like "And the nominees are..." run faster than the pictures can display? Martin Laracy took these problems head-on and solved them all.

I always marvel at how software engineers solve hardware problems. Martin Laracy at Compton's worked with the various elements of the data, sound, and pictures like an accomplished auto mechanic. Throw in a little of this, a little of that, adjust it, and it'll work. Then we had to test the multitude of different speeds of computers and CD-ROM drives that were in the marketplace, and make sure that it all ran properly on many kinds of computers.

While users of multimedia products see a product that hangs together if it's well-produced, many parts are working together behind the scenes. When users click on a mini-show in the Grammy disc, they see a show of pictures and sounds lasting 30-60 seconds. What the computer is doing, though, is running a long program averaging about a line of program for each second of viewing. It first puts something on the screen quickly, so the user has something to look at. While that screen is up, all the pictures, backgrounds for the pictures, the text that will appear on the screen, and other organizational information is moved to the hard disk. When that transition is complete, the first screen disappears and the program runs line by line, determining when to play what audio, when to display a picture, and how big to make letters on the screen. The audio always comes from the CD-ROM player, and everything else comes from the computer's hard disk.

When synchronization is involved—meaning more than one thing (pictures and audio) need to occur at once—the variations of computer hardware and software present an even bigger challenge. It is acceptable when products are not synchronized to click on a button and have a picture or a sound appear a second or a few seconds later, depending on the speed of the computer. You can then say, "Boy, this product is slow." However, it is not acceptable to watch a synchronized show of pictures and sounds that changes every 5 seconds as the Grammy disc does, and have the pictures or audio get off so that the sound comes up seconds before or after the picture. In that case you say, "There's something wrong here."

The diversity of computers and CD-ROM players in the real world presents a magnitude of possible speeds, and speed is a critical issue when synchronization is important. As Martin would say, "A computer or CD-ROM is only as fast as the weakest link." And there are a lot of places for weak links. There are differences in the seek times of CD-ROM drives (ranging from one-fifth of a second to over a second), in the transfer rate of a CD-ROM drive (150KB per second to 300KB per second to newer "double-speed" drives), in hard disk speeds (15 milliseconds to 60 milliseconds), and in computer "power" (from a 10MHz, 640KB RAM 286 to a 50MHz, 32MB RAM, 486). Then there's extended memory, expanded memory, and disk caching which users' computers may or may not have. The monitor might be a CGA, EGA, VGA, Super VGA, or the newer 24-bit monitors, and may or may not be standard. And of course in a PC world, there are versions of Microsoft Extensions, versions of DOS, versions of Microsoft Windows, and occasionally CD-ROM driver software that doesn't quite conform to specifications. Then if you want to use a sound board for more audio, there are MPC-compatible boards, and Windows-compatible boards, which may or may not be the same thing.

Somewhere in that smorgasbord, a product developer has to ask the basic question of what a product is and who it is being designed for. The easiest thing to do, and what pleases the hardware manufacturers and drives the sales of more computers, is to develop for the newest platform. This, though, can frustrate many users, because they bought a $69 CD-ROM product that requires a $199 board that needs to be installed by someone else. At the other extreme is to develop a product for the lowest common denominator, an older slower IBM AT or 286. This, though, can make it difficult to do many newer things, such as fast-moving pictures, that people seem to want.

Somewhere in the middle is a reasonable choice, and ultimately most multimedia developers produce multiple versions aimed at different major customer groups. Many people in the multimedia world fail to realize the difference between the installed base of computers and the number of computers shipping today. The installed base has absorbed eight years of shipping a bazillion different configurations, regardless of what's shipping today. Hardware shipped today, though of much better quality, still has many variations in an industry that is supposedly standardized. A multimedia proponent might see exciting technological advancement, yet a cynic could easily see an industry whose basic economic motive is perpetuating incompatibilities so new products can be sold to make make things work together, or for that matter, to work at all."

After months of work on our product we finally came up with a successful combination. It was fast enough, long enough, and worked on old and new computers. Martin also designed a language for easily tweaking the combinations as we discovered differences across machines, a language that was not much different from laying out a page on a word processing program. It was even something I could use to do some of the work myself.

The position of the multimedia aspects of the product posed another problem. Users of CD-ROM products have complained about CD-ROMs being weak in at least one of two areas: they either lack excitement or they lack substance. Information-oriented products tend to lack excitement, and multimedia products have generally been shallow, lacking substance or depth.

Multimedia products are usually either a non-interactive slide show, or a database with many sounds and pictures hidden and accessible by typing a word or browsing a list.

On the Grammy disc, we decided to make the multimedia slide shows as interactive as possible, so that at any time a user could "drop out" of the slide show to find more information about that year's show, or play a trivia game. In addition, we provided a full information database in which users could look up awards by artist, year, type of music, etc.

The result was promising. We built a fairly complex web of multimedia, information, and games that captivated the people who tested it for hours. With the goal to deliver creative excellence, we felt we had reached a point at which we could deliver a successful product.

The only negative feedback occurred when people momentarily forgot what they were looking at. Forgetting it was a computer, and these were digital pictures, they'd put the CD-ROM into the same league as television, remarking that it seemed a bit slow. This strange niche, between TV and computer databases, is an intriguing one that is being explored on the flip-side by interactive TV.

The next step was getting the product into customers' hands. With Compton's NewMedia distribution program, this was not difficult by 1992. The same Compton's distribution program that took on the Guinness disc in 1990 as its first outside product, carried over 150 products and was selling to 5,000 stores in 1992. Along with Sony, Compton's was the biggest distributor of CD-ROM products.

Building that distribution channel for CD-ROM products had taken a vision of the future—seeing CD-ROMs alongside books, records, and software as consumer products. Paul Bader, vice president of sales at Compton's, had taken an aggressive approach, believing that ultimately there would be only a few key distributors in CD-ROM as in other industries, and he wanted

Courtesy Compton's NewMedia

*Paul Bader, Vice President Sales for Compton's NewMedia, built a sales organization carrying 150 products through 5,000 stores. This made the distribution of the Grammy disc faster and simpler than with any previous product.*

Compton's to be one of them. Bader, a "man with a mission," had built an effective world-wide sales and distribution organization.

When the CD-ROM business started, I would've told you that our industry looked like the software business, with a few major distributors like Merisel and Ingram Micro D. Now I believe it is becoming just like the record business, without a passive distributor in between us and the stores, but instead we sell direct to a store. That's good, because we not only promote a product, we deal directly with the stores, so we're that much closer to the customer.

Paul, along with other Compton's executives, approached the market analytically, trying not only to determine who the customers were, but how to reach them. Today, he said, the number of channels selling CD-ROM is numerous. Software stores, hardware and software stores, mass merchandisers, consumer electronics stores, record stores, bookstores, video stores, office products, superstores, club channels, catalogs, college bookstores, are all places that Compton's sells its CD-ROM products.

"At the end of the day, though, only a few will really be able to sell it. There are a few general rules about who will win, such as "the consumer has got to see it." That makes stores that sell both hardware and software, or who are at least willing to set up the hardware, good choices. There are other channels we see as having great promise too, such as software stores which do not concentrate on video games."

Bader sees the buyers as being as dispersed as the sellers, ranging from the computer junkie to the "32-year-old Yuppie who needs a computer and CD-ROM for his kid because that's where education is going." Interestingly enough, Bader's view of the ultimate "Killer App" (short for killer application, or a real winner of a product) for CD-ROM is the one that Compton's made its name with—an encyclopedia. "You know, we've sold close to a million encyclopedias on CD-ROM," he said with pride.

Bader struggled from the sales side with the multitude of computer technologies, and how to sell to them. His view of the situation didn't leave doubt about who was at fault. "All the hardware manufacturers want to control the market like Nintendo did," he said. "It is the greed and avarice of the hardware manufacturers that most sets back the multimedia revolution today."

The great minds that conceived multimedia obviously wanted to make multimedia publishing easier. If only they had put the technology into the hands of the customers, the users, before the developers, we would have solved two problems. First, we wouldn't have to make computers do things they were never intended to, and second, we'd have feedback about what people want to see in these products. As it is, we have to push the limits of the computers, and really haven't gotten enough substantive market feedback.

When we were packaging the Grammy disc, someone pointed out that it was the first contemporary music CD-ROM. There were several CD-ROMs about Beethoven and classical music, but now we had a model for delivering contemporary music. That seemed odd—an industry whose roots were in the music business had forgotten the obvious thing that would make a good CD-ROM: music. With the ability to see and hear hundreds of favorite songs and learn more about them, the Grammy CD-ROM took a TV show and turned it into a multimedia show.

# nineteen

## All the News that Fits
## 1992

IT WAS A WARM SUMMER DAY AND I WAS AT THE WESTPORT, Connecticut city beach with Adam Pemberton, publisher of *CD-ROM Professional*. Adam's magazine had grown from being a respected library publication into the only stable magazine in the CD-ROM industry. The CD-ROM business was known for its high-profile nature and frequency of press coverage, but it was also infamous for failed magazines.

Adam and I were sitting in beach chairs discussing the "state of the industry." We'd done it often before—trying to pick who would be the winners and losers of the years to come. Adam usually had insights that I lacked, since he was inundated with information and could discern what was going to make it and what wasn't. I liked to temper my attitude about CD-ROM by intentionally keeping some distance from the mainstream, trying to concentrate on the "big picture." He was notoriously accurate for predicting the ultimate fate of other CD-ROM publications, and I felt that I had the same skill in predicting the future of CD-ROM publishers.

Adam and I got up and headed for his jet skis that we had already put in the water. I was nervous about trying jet skiing, having recently watched a television special about how difficult these engines-on-skis were to control. Adam had the build and skill to handle them, but right away I realized I was totally unprepared. I was surprised by how helpless I felt and we hadn't even started the jet skis yet.

He started the engines and gave me a few pointers about how to control these machines. He described how you let the jet ski drag you a little bit, then get up on your knees as you build a little momentum. Then he was off, and I watched him. In a few seconds, he was standing and gliding across the slick lagoon. I pulled the throttle slightly and decided to give it a try.

I gained some speed but was still unsure about how to get up on my knees. I tried one knee and then the other but it didn't work. I decided to do it like a horizontal pull-up, all at once. I was rocking a little, and both of my knees were just touching the top of the jet ski. Then I got up on both knees, pulled the throttle more, and suddenly felt like the Hulk with muscles ripping out of my skin, when—whack—I flew over the top of the jet ski. I found myself sitting on dry land next to the jet ski, seeing spots. Adam flew across the water, and pulled up next to me and stopped.

"You hit a sand bar," he said. "Are you all right?"

I sat awhile and collected my thoughts. All my apprehensions about jet skis had been confirmed in one short, 50-foot ride that ended abruptly. It was either swim back to shore or let the jet ski drag me, and I opted for being dragged. Back on the beach, we continued our talk about the CD-ROM industry from the comfort of our beach chairs.

I had gotten to know Adam and Online Inc., based in Southern Connecticut, through its ONLINE çonference, which had changed its name to ONLINE/CD-ROM. One year I distributed a flyer at the conference proclaiming "Publish Your Own CD-ROM." It invited people to stop by my table for a free appraisal of their idea for a CD-ROM. I'd then tell them, "It doesn't sound like something for CD-ROM," or "It's a perfect application of CD-ROM," or something in between. They didn't pay me a nickel, but I felt like Lucy from Peanuts.

In an industry as unstable as the CD-ROM industry initially was, it was important to have one rock-solid magazine to read for information on topics ranging from technical tips to industry news. *CD-ROM Professional* was able to publish topics of interest to a wide range of people in CD-ROM, without alienating any single group.

Most other magazines about CD-ROM have aimed at a particular niche in the industry. Perhaps that's the reason they didn't survive the lean years, because there just weren't enough readers of the type they were targeting. *CD-ROM Review*, appeared in 1986 attempting to reach the consumer market long before it existed. It was a surprise to go down to Long's Drugs and find *CD-ROM Review* on the shelf at a time when I still had to explain to 99 percent of the people I met what CD-ROM was. *CD Data Report* was an early entrant, and was the main vehicle in the mid-'80s for finding out what was going on in the CD-ROM industry. For smaller companies entering the CD-ROM field, though, the high subscription price for this industry newsletter was out of reach.

From the publisher of *CD Data Report*, Helgerson Associates, came *CD-ROM EndUser* in 1989. Though it targeted end-users, Linda Helgerson's usual sarcastic, direct tone came through. When I found too many bitter, hidden massages in her editorial content I called her to complain. I underlined the passages I didn't like, and asked her to explain. Among the more choice ones were the "sloppy first four years of CD-ROM," and that her publication was going to provide a "forum in which to vent frustrations toward those responsible for four-year-old inadequacies." The final straw was when she reviewed one of my company's products, and said, "It can be very frustrating to think, or know, that you have just been cheated or lied to and that who did it to you can do it to someone else." It sounded like a personal vendetta best saved for an industry-insider publication, not an end-user magazine. She didn't apologize, but she did provide some good evidence for the source of her frustration, if not the language that she used to describe it.

Later, Linda briefly published *CD-ROM Shoppers Guide* for the buyers of products, and *DISC*, which looked like a hybrid between her previous magazines: for industry people but looking like a professional magazine rather than a newsletter. Eventually, she decided to pull back and concentrate on the main publication that she was known for, *CD Data Report*.

*Digital Publishing* almost got off the ground in 1992. Rich Bowers was hired as editor but the magazine failed to make it to the market. Other magazines would surface briefly, then disappear, usually because they could not find a critical mass of readers. Publications had trouble reaching readers interested in CD-ROM since they were so dispersed.

Another niche of the market, covering "interactive video, multimedia, and related technologies" has been amply covered by the *Videodisc Monitor*, whose emphasis is on the videodisc with CD-ROM being one of the related technologies. Rockley Miller, the publisher of *Videodisc Monitor*, was also instrumental in starting a high-tech museum in Washington called Tech 2000, as well as the International Multimedia Association, which was born out of the International Videodisc Association.

*New Media* magazine and *MPC World* entered the scene in the early '90s to appeal to the multimedia aspect of CD-ROM. *New Media* attempted to attract the artsy, Macintosh-oriented readers, and *MPC World* looked like it had been funded by the MPC council to promote the MPC standard. Both magazines went through format changes early in their lives, and *MPC World* ended up folded into another larger magazine as a special supplement. *Publish!* a magazine known more for its coverage of tools and processes for information design, got a new publisher, Kent Ekberg. Ekberg had been in charge of Pioneer's jukebox CD-ROM, which contained six discs at the same time, and had covered CD-ROM in the context of information design. It was nice to see an "insider" from the CD-ROM industry in a key position.

In 1992, there were over 10,000 occurrences of the word "CD-ROM" in the press. Many people in the Western world read something about CD-ROM in 1992. CD-ROM "came out" in 1992, leaving its alternative lifestyle behind. Still, there are so many different opinions about what CD-ROM is, and what multimedia is, that publications are sparse. Proving how intangible and elusive professional CD-ROMers are, most publications that covered CD-ROM exclusively are out of business—except for *CD-ROM Professional, CD Data Report,* and the newer multimedia magazines.

Such is the treacherous world of CD-ROM magazines and jet skiing—just when you think you know what you're doing, you hit a sand bar, and are stopped dead in your tracks.

# twenty

## Twenty Years of Tennis, Anyone? 1993

If you played professional tennis in the last 15 years, you knew Benji Robins. Benji's name says it all—likeable, lovable, a curly head of hair, and easily hurt.

"What!" He'd yell whenever someone gave him a hard time, which they always did. He worked for the Association of Tennis Professionals, the ATP, the governing body of men's tennis, as a tour manager. He traveled 40 weeks a year to interesting and exotic places, meeting interesting and exotic people. And he had stories to tell.

There was the time he got a call from the band, Genesis, asking for tickets to the Wimbledon finals. They called the night before, and he pled their case to the Wimbledon committee the morning of the finals. Less than an hour before Genesis arrived, each in their individual limousines, Benji got the okay from the committee. In return, they invited him onstage at the closing concert of their European tour. He called me from all over the world, and brought back pictures of himself with tennis stars, as well as the likes of Brooke Shields and Christie Brinkley.

I've called Benji "Benjco" ever since he started talking about starting a business doing sports marketing. While he was at the ATP, we talked about putting their player handbook, which had pictures and biographies of the top players, on a CD-ROM. Benji sent me some slides, and we put together a prototype that sat around for several years. By the time I decided to pursue the idea more aggressively, Benji had left the ATP to go to business school at Kellogg in Chicago. He suggested several names to call, and I finally reached Byron Quann, the executive vice president of what was now called the ATP Tour.

After explaining the idea to Byron, he liked it. We planned to put 20 years of results, pictures, and biographies on CD-ROM. People could use the product to see pictures of past players, hear highlights from past years, guess who beat whom, and track players' careers. I did some quick arithmetic and figured we'd have the results of 100,000 matches, and surely we could figure something creative to do with that on a computer.

"Can you be down here day after tomorrow," Byron asked, taking me by surprise. It turned out they were having their 20th anniversary celebration and meeting, and it was a perfect time to get to know the ATP Tour and the people behind it. We laughed, and he prodded me by telling me not to think about it too much. I didn't, and the next day flew to Ponte Vedra Beach, Florida, the home of the ATP Tour.

As the airport shuttle dropped me off at the Marriott, a slender man walked past, not more than ten feet away, nodded a polite hello, and started jogging. I was a little shaken as I realized it was Bjorn Borg. He was almost a caricature of himself, like an aging athlete who was trying to look like Bjorn Borg.

I checked in and headed for the hospitality suite to encounter more legends of the past and personal heroes. Laver and Rosewall were there looking like they still enjoyed themselves as much as they had 20 years earlier. About 20 legendary players were in this little resort to play a seniors tournament being held in conjunction with the 20th anniversary activities.

The seniors, all past tennis greats, were struggling to keep their identities in a new atmosphere of fluorescent clothing and Andre Agassi. The senior tour was trying to mimic the success of the PGA, and came up with a "shoot-out" format—a fast-moving round robin in which players would play many opponents. It was supposed to make the play competitive and exciting to watch. It did create a lot of talk about where the senior tour fit, and garnered comments from the players that they had to warm up too fast, and the play was over too quickly.

I attended several days of seminars designed to give promoters, tournament managers, and tennis executives a feel for the present state of the game of tennis, and the future of the ATP Tour. Much talk centered on the ATP Tour, and its desire to attain the level of recognition of the NBA or PGA. There were some impressive statistics: 150 major world-wide events a year, the most visible sports body in the international arena, the high income of the spectators, and the clean and healthy image of the sport. It was the perfect environment in which to develop a CD-ROM, both to chronicle and promote the game. I thought about the Grammy Awards, which happened once a year. There were 150 regional tennis opportunities to promote this new product.

Brad Harris, the vice president of marketing and I seemed to be in sync, agreeing this new product was a great way to tie the past and the present together. Though filling tennis stadiums was the primary concern of the ATP Tour, there was a growing realization that the rich roots of tennis should not be forgotten. There was a fund-raiser honoring Arthur Ashe, with Bud Collins as emcee. The room was full of emotion as people from the past hailed tennis as it once was, toasting Ashe. Like some well-produced sideshow, Collins would begin a sentence only to be interrupted by a "Bud, Bud, excuse me, Bud," from the corner. Ilie Nastase would appear, try to make a joke, only to act as straight man for Collins or Vijay Armitraj, and by this time the whole room was in tears of laughter. Seeing Ashe, in his elegance and pride, was enough to make everyone catch their breath. I knew I wanted to do this product.

I presented the ATP Tour with a proposal to make the CD-ROM. As with any organization, they needed a reason for doing it. Though money is involved, often the non-money issues provide the impetus to get an organization on the CD-ROM bandwagon. With the ATP Tour, I tried to identify key elements that were important to them. They included:

- Generate enthusiasm for the game of tennis
- Present the ATP Tour as an organized body representing the game of tennis
- Act as an informational vehicle, for example telling people about upcoming tournaments so they can plan their travel accordingly
- Give the ATP Tour a chance to "tell the story of the ATP"
- Generate revenue for ATP Tour with no risk
- Archive and preserve an important part of the game of tennis
- Encourage the "cult-following" of tennis: tracking players and statistics as happens in a number of other major sports
- Merge the "classic" game of tennis with the newer "exciting" game of tennis

As I looked at that list later, a couple thoughts occurred. One was that I could almost substitute another organization's name and the list would hold up pretty well, especially if that organization was an association. For example, I could substitute

"NARAS" for "ATP Tour," and "music" for "tennis." And the list looked more and more like "communication," which was the essence of what we were trying to do with CD-ROM. Just like books, magazines, TV shows, radio, and movies, at the root of CD-ROM is a desire to communicate.

After months of negotiating, we signed a contract to produce an ATP Tour CD-ROM. It was the realization of a dream I had for years. Here was a chance to tie together the only two things I seemed to know in this world, but didn't seem to have any relation: tennis and CD-ROM. My choice was either to produce a CD-ROM about tennis, or try to play tennis with a CD. I was smart enough to choose the right one.

# twenty-one

## CD-ROM on Television and Television on CD-ROM 1993

RICHARD HART IS THE HOST OF A TELEVISION SHOW CALLED "The Next Step." Hart usually takes new high-tech tools and toys, and presents them in a short segment news format. Viewers see the next thing in high-tech electronics, medicine, travel, etc.

Richard Hart breezed past our booth at the Special Libraries Association conference in San Francisco. I was a little nervous because several years earlier, I had sent him a suggestion for a segment on, what else, CD-ROM. I had never heard from him, and hoped he wouldn't stop at our booth since I'd probably say something stupid like, "Did you ever get the letter I sent you?"

Special libraries specialize in certain subject areas, such as medical or legal libraries, and they are often internal libraries of large companies known as corporate libraries. I was standing in our booth, answering the usual questions about CD-ROM, when I felt a tap on my shoulder.

"Can you show us the Guinness Disc of Records," a harried man asked me. He had his show program out, and apparently had seen the Guinness name. "Sure, we have it here," I said. "What's it for?" "It's for Richard Hart," he said. "I'll be back in a few minutes with him and his crew."

Being on TV is everyone's hope and fear. I was usually calm with the press, but something about Richard Hart broadcasting locally, in my own backyard, gave me that dizzy, nervous feeling. I was reduced to feeling like a kindergartner at his first show-and-tell.

"Hi. I'm Richard Hart," a man said with a confident voice. He was stockier than I expected, and I realized that only his head was visible on TV. He went through a few minutes of setting up his cameras, surveying the booth for good photo shots, and asking some general questions. I resisted saying stupid things, hearing a voice, like the devil on my left shoulder, whispering, "Don't blow it."

"Let's get a shot of the disc being put into the CD-ROM drive," he said. "Can you just put it in there a few times?"

My hand, surprisingly, ignored my nervousness, and managed to place the CD into the drive many times, following his instructions. By this time, a small crowd had gathered, and my moment to make the ultimate sound bite was approaching. He asked me to stand a few feet back, look at him, and said he'd ask me some questions. In what seemed like a split second, he was right next to me, with a microphone, said "Look at me," and asked the first question.

"What are the most significant advances in CD-ROM in the past five years?" Asking me that question is like asking a priest to talk about the meaning of life. I would have been more comfortable responding to that question in front of a group of 5,000 screaming disbelievers than to him and the camera waiting for an instant remark.

I rattled off something about how easy it is now for anyone to use CD-ROM products, as opposed to needing the high level of skill they needed five years ago. The voice, the appearance, and the words were not me, they were another creature who had invaded my body just to remind me that I was not meant to be a TV star. The rest of the interview was a bomb that I quickly filed somewhere in my brain under "incompetence."

When the interview was over, Richard Hart took some more shots of the booth. As we were standing around, and the crew was packing up, I heard the same devilish voice inside me saying, "Go ahead, ask him."

"Did you ever get the letter I sent you?" I asked, all the while thinking, "What the hell are you doing?" After some discussion, he did, much to my surprise, remember the letter. Whew, I could leave that encounter with still a little of my pride intact.

Later, I realized that I had let the situation get out of control. I should've asked him what he was going to ask me, and taken a few minutes to think. I called my wife to tell her to watch the evening news. Neither my face nor my hand made the show, but it did open with a nice picture of our booth. Next time I am interviewed I'll do just like the booth and stand still, look nice, and keep my mouth shut.

As the conference continued, librarians of all specialties stopped by the booth—museum librarians, petroleum librarians, and pharmaceutical librarians. Most knew what CD-ROM was, though occasionally someone would ask in a derogatory fashion, "What is this CD-ROM stuff anyhow?" Usually that signaled they just didn't get it yet, and were begging someone to tell them what it was in a way they understood. A good way to get someone over this is to put a disc in their hand, have them put it in the CD-ROM drive, and tell them to watch the red light on the CD-ROM drive go on and off while the computer searches for something on the CD-ROM disc—ideally something they have typed in or selected.

Courtesy Journal Graphics

*Jim Hoffman, president and CEO of Journal Graphics, is turning a transcription company into a modern electronic information dynamo. Within two hours of broadcast, Journal Graphics has CNN available online. As well, many CD-ROM products are on the horizon.*

One man, looking out of place in a group of corporate librarians, stopped to inquire about our products. His badge said he was from Journal Graphics, which every avid television viewer associates with television show transcripts. "For a copy of the transcripts, call Journal Graphics," was something I had never done, but had seen advertised. I had also been thinking for a long time about putting television transcripts on CD-ROM, and as I found out, I wasn't the only one thinking about it.

Jim Hoffman introduced himself as the person who would be involved with any CD-ROM project of Journal Graphics. I was at first skeptical, since there was something contradictory about him: he claimed to hold executive powers at a well-known company, but he seemed too young, too nice, and didn't carry any of the stereotypical accouterments of an executive.

We spoke for the better part of an hour about putting transcripts on CD-ROM, and it turned out that Jim had been thinking of doing something similar. Journal Graphics owned the market in transcripts, turning spoken words into written words for the likes of "CNN," "Nightline," and several dozen other popular shows. Their motto, printed on a flyer he gave me, was "Television good enough to read." They transcribe 50 hours of television daily, a true feat. We parted by agreeing that I would visit their headquarters in Denver.

Several weeks later, I took that trip, with a bit of hesitation mixed with excitement, wondering what exactly this company did, and where Jim Hoffman fit. He met me at the airport, and after a short drive, we parked in what seemed like a small two-car city garage in a back alley. We walked in a back door, past mounds of boxes, and ended up in an older, charming three-story office building that obviously had more than two employees.

Jim told me more about the origins of Journal Graphics. Starting as a newspaper for the legal and law enforcement in New York City, in an area known as Journal Square, the company then became a typesetting service. Jim Smith, the founder of the company, came up with the idea of transcribing television shows after the company had been in business for five years. He himself transcribed the MacNeil-Lehrer newscast, then rode his bicycle downtown to try to sell the network on the idea the next day, transcript in hand. The network thought it was cute, but they didn't say yes until quite awhile later.

Television shows since learned that the idea is indeed cute or catchy, but it is also an effective way to promote a show and make money at the same time. Journal Graphics became the leader in this field by not only being good at transcribing, but also by establishing good relationships with the television networks. Now, Jim said, they were focusing on the new ways of distribution for the transcripts, and one key area was CD-ROM.

Jim was the real thing—a smart guy who held an authoritative position. As we sat in his oversized office, surrounded by high-tech devices and old desks, I glanced at the wall and saw a faded front page of a Washington newspaper. I got out of my chair, walked over and looked several times at the photo of the man holding a computer. It wasn't until I read the caption that I realized that it was a picture of Jim Hoffman. Though I didn't yet know the story behind this newspaper article, the puzzle of Jim's personality finally clicked—there really was something different about him. Before I got a chance to ask, his face changed into a reflective pose, and he started to talk.

"They really burned me," he said with a passion I hadn't seen. "Can you believe having a $15 million dollar company stolen from you?"

He spoke for awhile, and told me an incredible story that would probably have made most people change careers. It turned out that Jim had started a business named Seequa in Odenton, Maryland in 1982. It was a real up and comer, growing to $15 million in revenues in three years.

It seems that Seequa, one of the original clone manufacturers, had a line of credit called from their bank for no apparent reason other than the bank was getting nervous about the price drops in the clone market. The bank literally closed the company down and put the company's assets up for sale, asking Seequa employees to build as many computers as they could for an auction that would effectively shut down the company. Jim called the FCC and told them that the Seequa computers hadn't passed the FCC tests, and thus were illegal.

The picture from the paper was of Jim at the auction, his arm around one of the computers that couldn't be sold because Federal marshals closed down the auction. Almost a decade later, those computers are still in a government warehouse.

Jim didn't show any physical scars from the experience, but he had a certain toughness. We talked for many months before we finally came to an agreement to work together. We agreed to

# The Capital

ANNAPOLIS, MARYLAND, THURSDAY, JULY 25, 1985

## END OF LINE

### *FCC raid delays Seequa auction*

**By DEBRA VIADERO**
**Business Writer**

A discordant public auction at Seequa Computer Corp. in Odenton marked a fitting end to computer-making at the troubled firm.

Like a microcosm of the company's brief manufacturing history, the first day of public auctions at the plant was marred by conflict, bravado and financial disappointment for Seequa.

Trouble began 90 minutes before auction time when Federal Communications Commission officials and a federal marshal swooped in and seized $1 million worth of Chameleon model computers slated for the auction block.

The FCC charged that the 300 computers did not meet government standards for radio frequency emissions. The FCC maintains those standards so that radio waves from electronic equipment do not interfere with police and fire department communications, television or radio reception.

The raid — reportedly the largest in Maryland history — topped off a 10-month FCC investigation of Seequa. And, FCC officials said, it could lead to criminal charges against Seequa's executives. The FCC earlier this year fined the company $2,000 for continuing to market the high-emission Chameleon, said Maureen Perantino, a spokeswoman for the FCC.

Seequa executives, miffed at the surprise raid, denied all FCC charges.

Despite the interruption, the auction went on. Roughly 600 bidders from across the country came to buy valuable computers, production and testing equipment and office furniture at bargain basement prices.

Proceeds from the confiscated models — which were also auctioned off — were held in escrow. Chameleon buyers were told they could not take them home until the computers met government standards, an estimated 4-to-6-week delay.

Jim R. Hoffman, Seequa's vice president of marketing, said the FCC raid may have driven bids down.

(Continued on Page 12, Col. 3)

Photo by J. Henson

AGAINST A BACKDROP of roughly 600 bidders at a public auction yesterday at Seequa Computer Corp., Jim R. Hoffman, vice president of marketing for the company, rests atop a Seequa XT computer.

*Jim Hoffman, pictured here in 1985, leaning on one of the Seequa computers that the bank tried to auction before being stopped by the FCC.*

produce a series of products for both the consumer and media markets, giving many people instant access to a valuable source of information: transcripts. The transcripts would be combined with pictures and audio from television shows. Journal Graphics had recently obtained an exclusive agreement with CNN to produce transcripts around the clock.

In these days of sound bites, the transcripts from CNN proved to be very "meaty," containing extensive coverage from such events as the Democratic and Republican conventions, the presidential debates, various economic conferences, and of course, "Larry King Live." Transcripts, especially from cable networks where the news and interviews are longer, have the feeling of uncensored information. There is little opinion and few summaries in transcripts—they are mostly just what someone said about something. And CNN transcripts had full sentences and paragraphs, not just sound bites, which made for easier reading. This was in contrast to trends in network news, where the average appearance of a presidential candidate dropped from 43 seconds in 1968, to 8.9 seconds in 1992.

The Clinton campaign used the CNN transcripts effectively to manage the information flow of the campaign, searching daily in the Journal Graphics files online to see who said what the day before. CNN transcripts are available within two hours of broadcast. In addition to the Clinton campaign, hundreds of other media organizations, including newspapers, TV stations, and radio stations, all used the transcripts as important sources for stories. How else could you track what Ross Perot really said in 1992?

Jim Hoffman became the CEO and president of Journal Graphics during the months I got to know him. We continued to talk about the dozens of product ideas for the hundreds of thousands of pages of Journal Graphics transcripts. One day, Wink Saville suggested we do the Clinton Economic Conference.

Wink was a technical guru in CD-ROM publishing. He was one of the founders of Meridian Data, and built the software for the CD Publisher, the Meridian premastering system. I had talked with Wink before about the possibilities with transcripts on CD-ROM, and this idea seemed to be the catalyst to get the idea off the ground. We defined a product that would capture the before, during, and after of the conference. On Inauguration Day 1993, we sent a press release out to 2,000 sites with the headline, "Clinton Economic Conference on New CD-ROM." CNN agreed to participate in the project, which meant we could combine the transcripts with hours of audio and pictures to bring a new concept, "multimedia transcripts," onto CD-ROM. Wink was contracted to produce software that would mix transcripts with audio and pictures, so that transcripts would be brought to the foreground, appearing across the screen at the same time someone was speaking.

The day after the Inauguration, the *Wall Street Journal* seemed to like the idea of a Clinton disc being announced on Inauguration Day. On the front page, there was a small article that read, "Had enough of the Inaugural hoopla? Coming in March, the complete economic conference on CD-ROM disc from Journal Graphics." Though the wording poked a bit of fun at the importance of the disc, it was much better than not being mentioned at all.

What do Jim Hoffman and Richard Hart have in common, besides the fact that both walked unexpectedly into my life within an hour of each other one day?

Well, Richard Hart does a show on the Discovery channel, ideally about CD-ROM, but it really doesn't matter what the topic is. Jim Hoffman's company then takes Richard Hart's spoken words and puts them into writing. I then make a CD-ROM out of those transcripts, and sell it back to, who else but Richard Hart.

It's called the information economy. And it's here.

# twenty-two

## There's a Monkee on my Back
## 1993

WHEN SOMEONE FROM A COMPANY NAMED THE NEW RADIO STAR in Carmel, California calls about CD-ROM, you get an image in your head. It's probably some guy with a microphone in his basement, broadcasting late-night, low-budget shows to the hippies who never left Big Sur. But when Bob Hamilton said to me, "I think we can use CD-ROM as a way to promote major recording stars into radio," I listened.

In Carmel, I found a business that sold information. The New Radio Star sold information, news, gags, bits, and various esoterica to several hundred radio stations. Each morning, stations signed on to the New Radio Star online network and downloaded new stuff to use that day. Bob started the business ten years earlier.

Bob's fascination with CD-ROM began when he saw the Compton's Multimedia Encyclopedia at a conference in

Monterey, California. "I couldn't believe what I was seeing and hearing when I saw Compton's," he said. "It was the first time I had heard sound coming out of a computer. I went right home, called Compton's, and paid $795 for the disc."

"You know, my dad was a Methodist minister," he continued, "and he wore a double-breasted suit even when they went out of style. Though he was conservative, we were the first people in our town to own a television set. I was eight years old. Everyday, loads of people came over to watch TV with us."

"I feel the same way about CD-ROM now as I did about television then. I was the first person in our neighborhood to have a CD-ROM drive, and our neighbors have been coming over to see Compton's and the other products I've bought since, just like they used to come over and marvel at the TV."

I was as fascinated by Bob as I was by his business because he was the first person I'd met from the music business who talked my language. He remarked that I was the first person from CD-ROM who understood what he was talking about. He showed me some things he had done over his 35-year career. I was especially interested in an idea he had pioneered: the World Premiere. Bob would produce a World Premiere for a record company when one of their artists was coming out with a new record.

The World Premiere was a full package for radio stations to help them promote the artist. The package would include clips of songs, interviews with the artist, and cue cards with information on them about the artist. Bob did everything: interview the artist, produce the CD or LP with the interviews, and write the cue card. He had done this for everyone from Jefferson Starship to Gloria Estefan to George Strait. We quickly focused on a powerful concept: producing World Premiere CD-ROMs. They would be somewhere between what Bob already did and a television special. Not only would they sell, they would also promote the new releases on CD as well as catalogs of musicians, giving both the record company and musician an incentive to make a CD-ROM.

In the next several weeks, we wrote up the concept and presented it to several artists, all of whom were receptive. One day the phone rang at home and it was Bob.

"You want to have breakfast this weekend with Michael?" he asked. "I told him about you and he wants to meet you."

"Michael" was Michael Nesmith—a former Monkee and respected video producer, and also one of Bob's best friends. They had known each other since the '60s. Michael had moved to Los Angeles, but he still had an old family home near the center of Carmel, not far from Bob's place.

I drove down the following Saturday, picked up Bob, and we went to Michael's house. We went in the side door, and I was quickly introduced to Michael Nesmith, whom I never would've recognized. The only hint of a Monkee was a piece of paper taped to his refrigerator from a magazine making fun of the "Michael Nesmith hairstyle." The picture showed a much-younger Michael, his hair meticulously sliding over the middle of his forehead. I was also introduced to his girlfriend who quickly joined the conversation about CD-ROMs.

We sat around listening to Digital Music Express, marveling at how this might be the thing to send radio down the tubes. I had seen ads for this music service which came into the home in a similar manner as cable TV, but had not been impressed by the ads. This was the first time I had seen and heard it, and I was amazed at what it could do. You could program whatever style you wanted, and get non-stop music with no repeats. It was just like cable television, only it was just music with no pictures coming out of the TV. The conversation took on a significance for me, sitting there with two pioneers, talking about the future of music and radio. I hoped I could hold my own in this group.

We went out to lunch, and what started as a friendly visit suddenly became uncomfortable. Michael Nesmith hadn't smiled since I met him, and now I was being interrogated by him about my past. It elevated to a full-out attack, something I couldn't ever remember happening, and that I wasn't prepared for. My credibility was being questioned.

"How did you get into CD-ROM?" he'd asked. After each of my explanations, he said, "But I don't understand." I think he was expecting an MIT-educated, Hollywood-trained Yuppie. He was looking for my credentials, and I couldn't seem to satisfy him. When we got back to Bob's house, I showed him the Guinness disc.

"What did you do on this disc?" he said.

"The business I own, UniDisc, published it," I replied.

"But what did *you* do?" he asked impatiently.

I hesitated, and answered that I did just about everything—managing a team of technical and creative people who did everything from the packaging to the programming. He wasn't satisfied. He kept probing, wanting specifics.

"I see. You're kind of like an editor. You proof everything before it goes out the door," he said.

Thinking that if I kept going any longer he'd reduce me to being only the proofreader, I told him that yes, I was kind of like an editor.

We spent some time at Bob's looking at discs, then Michael left. I wasn't sure what had hit me, but I felt different. It was the first time in many years that my credibility had been questioned. I had asked him nothing about his past, since I thought it was inappropriate. I refrained from asking him if he ever really did take the "Last Train To Clarksville," because we were talking about CD-ROM. But that could have been a mistake.

Michael Nesmith was a pioneer, and was known worldwide for his work in video as well as music. He was trying to

*HEART, who made 13 albums and was nominated for four Grammy Awards, was excited by the CD-ROM World Premiere and retrospective concept, and gave the go-ahead. Pictured here are left to right, Denny Carmassi, Nancy Wilson, Ann Wilson, and Howard Leese, who are, together, HEART.*

figure out his relationship with this new medium called CD-ROM. He had met many of the "beautiful people" in the CD-ROM industry, the multimedia mavens of Hollywood. I probably didn't fit his model of what someone in my business should be like, because of my hands-on, sometimes cynical, view of technology.

Bob and I formed a new company, named the New CD Music Show with one mission: to produce music CD-ROMs based on major recording stars. The market for CD-ROMs with more and better music was heating up, and we wanted to combine our talents to get the most out of CD-ROM in this arena. The first people who were interested in what we were doing was the band HEART, who understood the significance of releasing a CD-ROM with a new record. Bob had done a World Premiere for them, and they invited us to Seattle to see them.

Ironically, the first project Bob and I completed was not a CD-ROM about a music star, it was just the opposite: an audio CD about a CD-ROM. It was the World Premiere of the Grammy Awards CD-ROM, and it went out to 1,200 radio stations. It was a fully-produced CD with music and sound from the Grammy Awards CD-ROM, designed for radio stations to play "Grammy Moments," run contests, or play interviews that had been pre-recorded about CD-ROM and specifically the Grammy Awards CD-ROM. All we asked of the radio stations was to credit the Grammy Awards CD-ROM anytime they played something, in the same way they'd credit a music artist. For the first time we know of, radio was "playing our song" from a CD-ROM. We had reports from all over the country that it was being played, and close to 50 stations ran contests to give away the actual Grammy Awards CD-ROM to its listeners the week before the 1993 Grammy Awards.

Besides using CD-ROM products, there are many opportunities in the publishing and production of CD-ROMs for people in the music business. CD-ROM gives music professionals a new medium in which to use creative skills and find new markets for music. Since the main element that turns a computer into a "multimedia" computer is the addition of sound capabilities, the need for quality sound production will continue to increase. As people move away from a gee-whiz attitude when they hear music coming out of their computers, their expectations for quality production will increase. The same thing will happen in homes, when the initial enthusiasm over being able to interact with a television set passes.

Specifically, many skills used to create videos or television commercials are needed in CD-ROM. The audio needs to be recorded, edited, mixed, and mastered—the only difference is in the capabilities of the playback system: a CD-ROM instead of a VCR or television.

In addition, licensing of music to CD-ROM publishers creates a residual royalty stream for music publishers resulting in additional revenue for music that has already been recorded. Music might be used as background to enhance a mood, or as specific pieces that play a higher profile in the product, and or might be the central piece. Publishers of CD-ROM products usually have a fixed percentage of product revenue that can be allocated to royalties, and the audio portion shares that with any other licensed pieces, including photos and text.

Many of these areas, where particular services are contracted for, are driven by the budget of a CD-ROM project. Budgets to produce new CD-ROM products can range from under $25,000 to well over $1 million. There are still some companies in the CD-ROM business that consider it a luxury to use music professionals, but most are coming to understand the value of using an expert.

Another opportunity for music professionals is original CD-ROM production, where the disc is produced from beginning to end by someone from the music business. With few exceptions, CD-ROMs are built by finding compelling text and pictures, and adding audio for enhancement. CD-ROMs published by members of the music industry might assume a different appeal, and bring a better understanding of the use of audio in an "interactive multimedia" environment. A top-notch computer programmer is still needed to mix all the elements and make sure a CD-ROM has technical integrity, since the production tools often involve writing computer programs to control the interaction with the user.

Possible CD-ROM products that feature music are endless. The use of audio on computers has gotten a bum rap because of its low quality. Home video games, arcade games, and computers have driven many parents and friends crazy with a steady stream of "beeps and boings." That sound can now be replaced by high-quality music.

Photo courtesy of Sony

*Writable CD-ROM drives, or "one-offs", are impacting both the CD-ROM and music business for their ability to quickly produce a CD. Current models are simple additions to computers, as pictured here, and cost less than $10,000.*

Recently writable CDs or "one-offs" have affected both the CD-ROM and music business. They are being used today to make demo CDs in recording studios, and are also used heavily (with a little software added) in the testing and prototyping stage of CD-ROM production. With CD-ROM, there are many elements at work, and significant testing is required on a new product to make sure there are no bugs. Cutting a sample disc to send to someone to review and test is invaluable. The devices that make these discs have dropped below $10,000, from $100,000 in 1989, and the discs are around $30 each. Some companies with such machines have set themselves up as CD-ROM service bureaus, and will press a one-off disc for a fee.

The CD-ROM and music business are joined at the hip, and need each other to grow in the industry. Nearly all the record and movie companies created groups or divisions in 1992 to produce "new media." Other announcements, like Warner's announcement about the availability of 30-second clips of some top-name artists for use on CD-ROM products, further sparked a hybrid industry—one taking advantage of the technology of the computer industry and the creativity and resources of the entertainment business.

Soon we'll no doubt see the latest horror flick, "I Was A Teenage Hollywood Propellerhead," coming to a virtual reality theater near you.

# twenty-three

## Hippies, Yuppies Catch Multimedia Fever 1993

ONE SATURDAY MORNING I ATTENDED AN INFORMAL MEETING OF residents of Santa Cruz County. Tentatively calling ourselves the Multimedia Moguls, we were a group of six people who were assembled by two local people, Sheridan Tatsuno, an expert on Japan–U.S. technology exchange and author of *Created in Japan*, and Mike Leahy who ran an office for a company that produced DVI software. Besides the three of us, there were a computer programmer, video producer, and someone else—I'm not sure what he did but he couldn't stop talking about the HomeBrew club that started the computer culture in the Silicon Valley in the '70s. He thought this group of Moguls was going to be the same thing, but for multimedia—he seemed to be looking for something that had been missing in his life since HomeBrew had been abandoned.

All of us had hidden agendas, and mine was that I wanted to find more talented people locally to work with. Sheridan had a much more ambitious set of goals—he wanted to set up a multimedia center in the middle of Santa Cruz, and to make it part of the rebuilding of Santa Cruz, a combination technology center, artist's colony, and tourist attraction.

We met every few weeks until the group had grown to about 25 people, and we were meeting at a coffee shop. I felt a sense of brotherhood with this eclectic group, people who shared an interest in emerging technologies and their applications. We were having our coffee one morning when a newcomer stood up to talk.

"This is really a happening place," he said. "I can feel that we're all working together to get the planet back into shape."

A silence fell over the talkative group, and then another person stood up. "I agree. Santa Cruz has always been a spiritual center, and this is just an extension of what happened here in the '60s." The air shifted, and I felt uncomfortable.

What happened in Santa Cruz in the '60s is not that different from anywhere else except for two things: the intensity and the length of time. The '60s never left Santa Cruz. Santa Cruz was, and still is, a very left-leaning town, and proud of its ability to hold onto its '60s dreams. That can be the beauty of living there, but sometimes it can also rub you the wrong way. After all, any philosophy taken to an extreme, regardless of how liberal it is, can be confining.

The Multimedia Moguls changed and what started out as a multimedia chamber of commerce became a group therapy session. The people who had been at that first meeting were out, and the new regime was in. The next meeting was held at Digital Media, a company owned by Dan Mapes, the man who initiated this change to save the planet. It had a decidedly different flavor. Finding new connections between multimedia and the world's problems started many conversations that ultimately resulted in talk about the problems themselves: cleaning up the environment, social inequality, the educational crisis. We sat in a semicircle, the group having grown to 50, and someone announced that the group was now the Multimedia Maestros.

When we weren't talking about changing the world, the talk was mostly about "raves"—all-night parties full of music and dancing if you talked to the participants, and full of sex and drugs if you listened to the media reports. All raves, though, had a form of live multimedia, and the new leader of the Maestros made most of his money putting on multimedia events for raves. Cynics talked about the multimedia shows as nothing more than gentrified light shows of the '60s, whereas, the creators thought of it as a new form of artistic expression, ultimately linked with virtual reality—the high-tech emotional high of the future. Instead of doing drugs to get into a new dimension, the raves of the future would accomplish this with computerized headgear that took you there, somewhere, instantly. Somehow I couldn't incorporate raves into my framework for multimedia.

An unusually large number of CD-ROM people live or work in Santa Cruz County. At the store, at the beach, and at the movies, I often run into someone from the CD-ROM industry. This could be just coincidence or it could be a sociological phenomenon, but I see evidence daily of the existence of a CD-ROM and multimedia subculture living on the coast of California.

Sony Electronic Publishing is in Monterey and if you had your traffic-cam on Highway 1 each morning, you'd see a southern migration of ex-Meridian Data people each morning heading for Sony. As the need for Meridian's publishing products decreased and CD-ROM publishers learned to make their own home-grown versions of the Meridian product, many Meridian people left and went to Sony.

Greg Smith, a unique combination of engineer and salesman, was the first to head south, and was hired as general manager for the Sony group. Soon a flood of people were hired from

Meridian, though Greg was very careful. Meridian was fuming about the hemorrhage of people, so Greg took ads in the local newspaper, the *Santa Cruz Sentinel*, and didn't approach a Meridian employee directly unless they responded to an ad, or independently contacted Sony. Since Sony had become the primary manufacturer of CD-ROM Write-Once devices, which Meridian bought and resold, Meridian and Sony had to maintain a cordial relationship for the sake of both businesses. Many talented people joined Greg, including Francis Juliano, Dean Quarnstrom, and Dave Hoshaw.

The official word in Meridian's customer newsletter said, "Greg Smith, vice president sales, resigned Meridian to pursue other interests. His boundless enthusiasm and quick wit will be sorely missed. Greg will no doubt be a success at whatever he chooses to pursue and we wish him the best in the future." However, when Meridian found out he'd gone to work at Sony, the tide turned. A high-level Sony executive received a terse legal letter from Meridian saying, "We have been informed as recently as yesterday that your proselytizing of our employees through your direct and indirect channels is continuing. We need a commitment from you to cease and desist...." Sony's response was to point out that Greg left Meridian two months before he joined Sony, that he was one of 500 people who responded to ads in the *San Jose Mercury*, and that many people from Meridian had contacted Sony even before Greg arrived. By this time, it was too late because the power base for CD-ROM had already shifted from Scotts Valley to Monterey.

"Hey, I'm a good recruiter," Greg Smith said to me after it happened. "I recruited about a third of the people who worked for Meridian. There's nothing wrong with placing an ad in the *Sentinel* that has two key words in big, bold letters: CD-ROM and Sony."

The Sony group took on all parts of the CD-ROM industry. They worked closely with their Japanese counterparts, developing software for new products such as the Data Discman and the MMCD. Also coming out of this group were an affiliated label program, in which they would distribute other companies' products in the retail market. They also developed specialized applications, including the Mayo Clinic disc and the Particle Atlas. Soon their focus also included games.

Although they were right up the street, I was never able to develop anything more than a friendship with the people there. It was probably because everyone wanted to do business with them. They were bombarded with good ideas, and had trouble choosing what to work on. In all their activities they followed a fairly rigid way of doing business that ultimately put most of the risk on the other companies, like mine. When they put their business models on the board, there didn't seem to be a place for UniDisc. I assumed that part of their success was getting other companies to do business, with the outside companies shouldering much of the risk.

In early 1993, Greg Smith made another move, leaving Sony and forming his own company to publish CD-ROM discs. Many of the people who had left Meridian for Sony followed him again. Included in that group was Francis Juliano, who had been a key person at both Meridian and Sony, and Arthur Mrozowski. Arthur had been also begun his own company on the side named CD-ROM Galleries, which produced "art gallery" discs that featured photographic works of art. The new company Smith, Juliano, and Mrozowski formed acquired CD-ROM Galleries as its start. About the same time, Bob Headrick, who had hired Greg, also left Sony to become president of Nimbus Records, one of the major CD mastering facilities. Once more the California coastal CD-ROM culture was shaken up by these moves, and no one was quite sure where it was all going to end.

The "CD-ROM culture" has gathered a smattering of people from the library, corporate, publishing, software, and entertainment worlds. It is its own unique group of people interested in using CDs for new and exciting things. It remains to be seen if the "CD-ROM" and the "multimedia" cultures will ultimately mesh. After all, to people in both cultures, text, sound, and pictures are all the same thing...they're all just data. It's just that the prominence of, for example, sound in the multimedia world, is of higher importance than in the library world, where the use of sound, with or without headsets, is still a controversial subject.

I'll never forget the dinner I attended after another speech at SIGCAT in Washington. At the dinner was Jerry McFaul, as well as Randy Jackson, brother of Michael, and Taylor Kramer, vice president for UVC Corporation and the former drummer for the rock group Iron Butterfly. What else but CD-ROM would bring these people together in one room? Kramer's company had developed some new technology for putting full-screen video on a computer, and Jackson was a combination spokesperson and vice president of entertainment. Together they had formed a unique partnership to use this technology for educational purposes that they were promoting through SIGCAT.

This partnership, named JEdI or Joint Education Initiative, was a pioneering effort in conjunction with the University of Maryland and other government agencies. JEdI provided teachers and students with scientific data and image display programs from such widely disparate sources as Yellowstone Park, the Voyager space photos and data, and the ozone layer. It included a teacher's activity book. Randy Jackson made a convincing speech at the SIGCAT meeting that day describing his boredom with school, and how enthusiastic he was about programs like JEdI for keeping kids in school. JEdI was a concerted effort to use CD-ROM as a real teaching tool, rather than just a data distribution method.

After the success of the Silicon Valley, both the name and the place, it only made sense that geographic areas would compete for being the center of CD-ROM and multimedia activity. Washington and New York had far more CD-ROM publishers until the late '80s when "multimedia" publishers began appearing in the traditional locations of Los Angeles and Silicon Valley. The exact center of the industry, though, shifted with the announcements of new products from various parts of the country.

The media, looking for a new angle on the multimedia explosion, focused on a ten-square block area of San Francisco where artists, programmers, designers, producers, and hangers-on were congregating, creating a self-styled multimedia heaven. This area, tagged Multimedia Gulch, was the place to be, much like Silicon Valley when it started. The image of San Francisco and the image of multimedia were consistent, they said, down to the last drop of double-espressos.

Just like the Multimedia Moguls/Maestros were caught up in themselves, and the excitement of belonging to something new and innovative, Multimedia Gulch looked not like the Haight-Ashbury of decades ago, but like the Yuppies of recent history. It became unfashionable to be a Yuppie when money became the social ill of the '90s, but if you are a multimedia Yuppie that seems to work. Unemployed Silicon Valley workers can take off their pocket protectors, don a beanie, and venture north to Multimedia Gulch to try make money without an ounce of guilt.

These hybrid social/technological changes are inevitable, and when there is general agreement about what multimedia is—if it's really just CD-ROM renamed or something more akin to a religion, then the geographic center will become apparent. After all, who would've ever thought that Missouri would compete with Nashville as the center of country music. These things change.

No matter what city or what group ends up steering the industry, you can be sure that there will be a migration to Multimedia City unlike anything seen before.

# twenty-four

## CD-ROM is Open for Business 1993

In an alley named Peter's Lane, near the Smithfield meat market in North London, is a company named Task Force Pro Libra, Ltd., or TFPL for short. In 1986, TFPL published the first comprehensive directory of products and companies in the CD-ROM industry. It contained 48 products and was called the *CD-ROM Directory*.

TFPL is run by Nigel Oxbrow, who built the company from its origin as a placement service in the information profession. Nigel's assistant, who handled the *CD-ROM Directory*, was a pert, quick and opinionated woman with strawberry blonde hair named Hilary Lambert. She had been an art major in college, and had mixed feelings about the information profession, which sometimes seemed a bit slow-paced.

The *CD-ROM Directory* was sold only as a book until we reached an agreement in 1990 that UniDisc would produce a CD-ROM version. "Makes sense," everyone seemed to say, and I agreed. The book had grown to some 800 pages, and had many indexes in the back to help find information about products.

Now I found myself formally at the center of the industry, whereas before I had informally been hooked in. Previously, I had been asked to provide people with ideas and projections, and now I was looking to the past and to the present to quantify and qualify what had happened. Working with existing information, instead of speculating, was refreshing. I also realized that there was a legitimate history to the emerging CD-ROM industry, given five or six years of experience and information to look back on.

I found myself deluged with information about new products because the publishers wanted to be in the directory, which didn't cost them anything. I accumulated that information and sent it to TFPL, who then sent "chasers" after the companies to obtain specific information from a structured questionnaire. Every six months the information was edited and sent back to us to produce a CD-ROM.

The challenge of producing an international directory became evident as we began discussions with TFPL regarding the right "English" to use on the disc. Should it have "British" English or "American" English, and what effect would these decisions have on the U.S. market? TFPL wanted to keep the British English and promote it as a truly international directory. I suggested that most people in the U.S. thought the world ended at U.S. borders, and buying an "international" directory was not something most people wanted to do.

Then we had to decide who this directory was for: was it an industry directory for the people whose main business was CD-ROM, or was it for the guy who just bought a CD-ROM

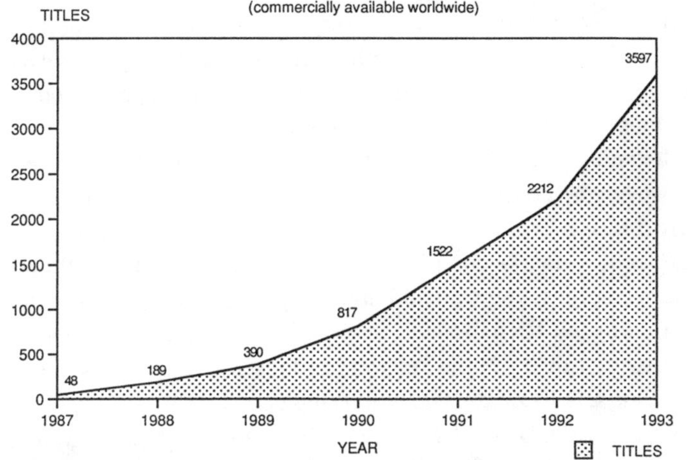


*The number of CD-ROM titles has about doubled each year since the first year CD-ROM products were available.*

drive and wanted to find out what other products were out there? We decided it was for a combination of industry people, professionals and librarians, and for consumers who were on the serious end of CD-ROM.

The directory contained more than 2,000 products, usually what we heard over the phone was, "Are there *that* many products?" As that number increased by over 50 percent per year, the task of collecting the information became more complex. In addition, the terminology began to change, and words like "multimedia" and "CD-ROM XA" entered the language, and had to be defined correctly so users could find information on "multimedia" products quickly. I always maintained that we were the only ones in the world forced to define "multimedia," and rarely were we 100 percent comfortable with this word of many faces.

Then there was the issue of the outside packaging. Should we make it look like the book, bright red with black letters? Should we give it a U.S. appeal, with lots of color and reasons to buy the product on the outside? Or should we be stereotypically British, conservative and understated? Everyone had a different point of view. The result at first was all of the above, and no one was entirely happy. On succeeding versions, the only common ground we found was to make the disc look exactly like the book.

Statistics about the CD-ROM industry are hard to come by. However, by consulting the *CD-ROM Directory*, and gathering information from the Optical Publishing Association and Infotech, a nearly complete picture of the past, present, and future emerges. The Optical Publishing Association, run from its beginning by Rich Bowers, tracks disc manufacturing, while Infotech, run by Julie Schwerin, does a once-a-year study detailing CD-ROM disc sales and shipments.

Over 3,000 CD-ROM titles are available for purchase today, and about 2.5 million CD-ROM drives are installed worldwide. Approximately 20 percent of the CD-ROM titles include some form of sound on the disc. CD-ROM discs are available in just about every language and country in the world. A successful title today ships between 10,000 to 25,000 units, with most selling below that mark. Infotech puts the size of today's worldwide market for CD-ROM titles and hardware at $2.5 billion. Most of the revenue cited in the Infotech report is from commercial, professional, and library products since the consumer segment is relatively new.

The OPA collects disc replicate numbers from the mastering facilities, but does not release these numbers—though there is continuing industry pressure to do so. The OPA does release percentage changes, and the change from 1990 to 1991 was a 95 percent increase in CD-ROM masters and a 250 percent increase in disc replicates.

Most parts of the CD-ROM business are growing at 50 to 100 percent per year, but as that growth occurs the obligatory "shakeout" is apparent. Many companies that invested money in the mid-'80s just couldn't hold on while the market expanded. Early press reports created a flurry of enthusiasm over CD-ROM based on prototypes at trade shows, only to come back several years later and pronounce CD-ROM dead. Much of this information did not serve the public well, and contributed to a general confusion about the CD-ROM industry and what it was trying to do.

As we produced several issues of the *CD-ROM Directory*, I began to like the TFPL people and we seemed to have a genuine friendship that exceeded our business relationship. Early on, advertising for our product was refused by *CD-ROM EndUser* because the publisher, Linda Helgerson, my best buddy on the day I started my business, said it competed with a product of hers. Apparently we had entered her kingdom, unwittingly. We just found advertising elsewhere.

We mailed a flyer announcing a new issue of the *CD-ROM Directory*, and two weeks later I received an almost identical flyer from a company named the Myriad Group in Florida. It was advertising a product named the *CD-ROM Directory*. I phoned and reached the president of that company, who claimed it was all accidental. Myriad was just coming out with a new newsletter on multimedia edited by a former *San Jose Mercury* columnist whom I had never met, but I had missed her trendy columns since she stopped doing them, Denise Caruso.

We looked over Myriad's flyer and the more we looked, the more identical it was. We studied our past phone records, and found they had called frequently over the past months requesting information—so much for accidents. I called back and got a guarantee they would change the name of the product and make sure anyone ordering their product knew what they were ordering, and that ours was available. Theirs, at $49 contained 300 companies and products, and ours at $149 contained 3,000. Hilary, with a little Sherlock Holmes in mind, called the company to order a copy, so she could see what they said. Her British accent coming on the day of my discussion with them didn't fool them.

After four issues of the *CD-ROM Directory*, Hilary called one day to tell me she was going to Africa for a year. Coincidentally, I had decided it was time to move on, since I enjoyed doing new products more than updating existing ones. We had our first discussion on how to part ways. We hadn't figured out how to do it yet, when an article appeared in *PC Magazine* and mentioned the *Directory*. The same week the *Wall Street Journal* called and soon a small article appeared on the front page. We were deluged with calls about a product we were getting out of, and had agreed not to sell. It was the busiest week we'd ever had—seems like my timing could've been better.

The *Wall Street Journal* article prompted several calls asking if we were a public company. When we said we weren't, the next question asked if there was a public company in the CD-ROM business, whose only business was CD-ROM. Again, I answered no.

The *Journal* article quoted a 60 percent increase in the number of CD-ROM titles in 1992, which came from me, but its headline stated "CD-ROM titles surged in 1992, but is a wider market at hand?" I compared the tone of that article to the first article in the *Journal* in 1985, and decided its level of enthusiasm had remained steady, not too positive or negative. It had, though, switched from spelling "disk" to "disc." I looked further down the article, and there it was—a quote from Denise Caruso who was "skeptical that CD-ROMs are at the brink of a big consumer market." I did a quick reality-check and realized we were ending 1992, and wondered if skeptics were just something I'd have to learn to accept. Maybe my expectations were too high.

Then I glanced at the cover of the *PC Magazine*. In welcome, easy-to-read letters, it proclaimed, "27 Reasons To Buy a CD-ROM Drive Now."...progress.

# twenty-five

## CD-ROM is Here—Now!

## 1993

CD-ROM HAS AFFECTED JUST ABOUT EVERY PART OF BUSINESS—entertainment, manufacturing, government, education, and publishing. The list of industries that do *not* have CD-ROM products is now very short.

Just in the Bay Area, many people from vastly different disciplines are struggling with the same issues. They have many good things that will fit on a CD-ROM—now they have to figure out exactly what to put on the disc, to how to get it there, and what the disc should look like on the outside.

South of San Francisco, Aircraft Technical Publishers is putting its aircraft maintenance information on CD-ROM for aircraft mechanics to have instant look-up for parts while they're working on an airplane. Down the road a bit is Electric Power Research Institute, which sends research reports and electric

*Shepard Broadfoot, a character, left NewsBank but is still in CD-ROM, representing Buckmaster Publishing in selling its CD-ROM products.*

power data to hundreds of electric utilities on CD-ROM. A little further south Sociometrics is using CD-ROM to distribute research studies about social issues, and investigating a CD-ROM game for helping to teach teens about teenage pregnancy. Across the Bay, Microdataware is marketing its new CD-ROM to everyone from companies with clean rooms to police departments, for identifying particles under a microscope. And that's just within driving distance.

Head to Southern California and you'll find World Library has put over 1,000 of the great books on a CD-ROM, from Aristotle to Aesop. To enhance your trip back in time with the greatest books ever written, pick up the Beethoven String Quartet from Warner New Media

Then hop on a plane to the East Coast, and find R.R. Bowker which has put its classic Books in Print on CD-ROM, and is selling it to bookstores. The *New England Journal of Medicine*, over five-years worth, is now on a CD-ROM. Jack Speer at Buckmaster Publishing in Virginia put 500,000 ham radio call signs on a disc, for ham radio operators. Jack, who was formerly a vice president at NewsBank, also produces a news product called Front Page News that competes with NewsBank—handling sales and distribution for Front Page News is none other than Shepard Broadfoot. While you're back East, don't forget to take a look at the thousands of discs produced by the government—and the clip art and photo discs, the game discs, and the typographical discs.

The international community is involved in CD-ROM, too, with Italy playing a major role because CD-ROM helped it get over some inefficiencies in its phone system. In Germany and the United Kingdom as well as every other country in Europe, CD-ROM is a big hit. And what about the SVINGA product detailing the country of Zimbabwe? Best of all would be to go to Hong Kong, and buy Great Cities of the World from InterOptica. Then you can use the CD-ROM for "virtual travel."

CD-ROM is even made for your coffee table at home. *From Alice to Ocean* is an attractive coffee-table book, packaged with a CD-ROM that includes the author's spoken comments, and a graphic map detailing the voyage. Time-Warner made a book and CD-ROM combination with photos of the Clinton campaign. And *American Style* is a book with pictures and descriptions of products that are classically American, written by author and photographer Richard Sexton—we licensed it several years ago but it sat on the shelf while we tried to decide if there was a market for these fun and informative books. Much to my surprise, a full-page ad in *Newsweek* appeared for the *From Alice to Ocean* book, and it is selling in local bookstores, complete with CD-ROM tucked in. Bookstores selling CD-ROM, albeit hidden in the inside jacket, is a reality.

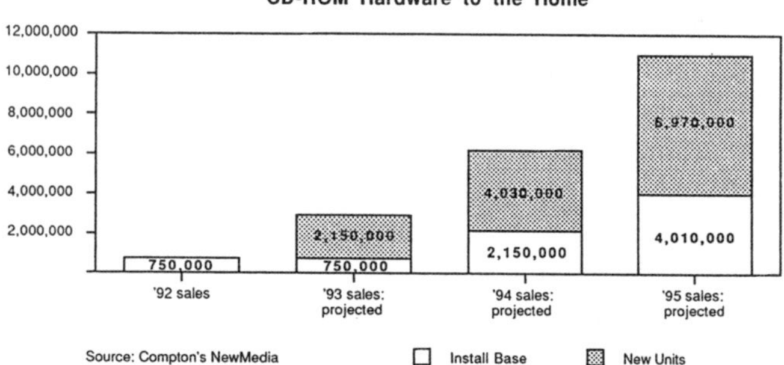


*Projections are that over ten million CD-ROM, or CD-something, units will be in consumers' homes by 1995.*

The real people who will benefit from CD-ROM are today's children. Instead of looking at the boob tube, they can have as much or more fun and learn at the same time. Instead of swallowing all that comes across the television screen, they can communicate and interact with stimulating products. Can you imagine what a public television documentary on endangered species would be like if every time an animal appeared on the screen the viewer, or user as we call them in CD-ROM language, could stop the documentary and ask questions?

What will happen in the future? With CD-ROM, projecting the future is easy because the future is now. It is happening—though it is still a moving target. CD-ROM is the thing of the present and it's here to stay.

Advances will continue on all fronts, making the technology easier to develop, as well as easier to buy. There will be the usual drop in prices, increase in speeds, growth of storage capacities, and shrinking data.

In the next decade, my crystal CD tells me that some other events will occur too:

- Videotapes will be replaced by CD-ROMs, though the exact acronym of that CD-ROM has yet to be seen—no more broken tapes. After several years of just transferring movies to CD-ROM, original movies will emerge designed to take advantage of the interactivity of CD-ROM.
- Making your own CD or CD-ROM will be like making your own cassette or copying information to a floppy disk.
- "Multimedia" will be replaced with a less generic term specific to the uses of CD-ROM—something like "computer movie."
- Good CD-ROMs, like really good books and movies, will be few and far between. The industry will continue to grow by repurposing existing works, instead of creating original products.
- Despite all the multimedia mania, the largest sector of growth for CD-ROM will continue to be traditional CD-ROM products that are information-intensive. That is, of course, unless John Naisbitt writes another book telling us we're now moving from an information society to an entertainment society. In that case, multimedia wins, and all bets are off.
- Sometime near the end of the decade, when homes have the right computer hardware installed, CD-ROM publishing will be one of the fastest growth industries.
- A CD-ROM drive will be built from scratch specifically for CD-ROM, instead of trying to enhance an audio CD player.
- After lots of soul searching, failures, and angry customers, original uses of CD-ROM will emerge to excite customers.
- The lure of CD-ROM will bankrupt many companies.
- The inherent strength of CD-ROM will make many companies rich.
- The plastic jewel case will be replaced by a more durable packaging that is as visually attractive as the CD itself.

- Federal Express will make a special shipping pack for sending CD-ROMs.
- Many people will discover that CD-ROM is fun and won't be afraid of it.

Kids who grow up with CD-ROM will take it for granted, which is the best thing that could ever happen. Instead of paying attention to the technology, they will look at what's inside, in the same way they read a book for the content, instead of paying attention to the physical delivery of the information. The really amazing products will be made by the kids who grow up with CD-ROM, and decide they want to make their own.

When kids grow up and make their own CD-ROMs, they won't have to worry about many things that get in our way today. They won't have to make pictures smaller so they can be taken off the CD-ROM drive fast enough. They won't have to, I hope, decide which XYZ version of which ABC platform is winning the technology race, because the market will demand better cooperation among manufacturers, and more permanent decisions about new versions of software. They will be able to easily move an idea from its inception onto the desks and into the living rooms of people who are ready and willing to use CD-ROMs.

In the next generation, maybe everyone will realize what CD-ROM really is. It's the only thing that humanizes that off-white, make-you-squint, cold sheet-metal contraption called a computer. If the CPU is the brain of the computer, then CD-ROM is its heart.

What, then, is at the heart of CD-ROM? People. Millions of people, all over the world, enthusiastically making and using CD-ROMs—with all their hearts.

# The People's CD-ROM Glossary

**access time:** How fast the CD-ROM drive can read the disc. For multimedia discs using lots of pictures and sound, a CD-ROM drive with a fast access time is needed, usually less than 300 milliseconds, or about a third of a second.

**application:** How something is used—a legal application or a medical application or an entertainment application, etc.

**audio:** Usually means music, but can mean speech, sound effects, or any sound.

**authoring software:** Software that is used to build CD-ROM discs. It's equivalent to a combination word processor and spreadsheet on a computer. About 100 companies license CD-ROM authoring software.

**Board**: A piece of hardware installed in the computer to make it do something new.

**Boolean:** A way of finding information on a computer by using "and" and "or" and some other words like "but not." For example, if you wanted to find information on "tall trees," you'd type "tall and trees."

**bundle:** Packaging a CD-ROM, or whatever, along with something else so you get a CD-ROM, or something else, for free. With a bundle, when someone buys a CD-ROM drive, they get some CD-ROM discs to use. Now, if only they would learn how to bundle batteries with flashlights.

**byte:** A small amount of information stored on a computer, usually equal to a single letter of the alphabet. To understand large amounts of information, *see* **Megabyte.**

**CD:** The audio disc that killed the LP record. Stands for compact disc.

**CD-I:** A consumer version of CD-ROM, designed to be connected to a television set and made popular by Philips. Short for "Compact Disc-Interactive."

**CD-ROM:** A compact disc, just like the CDs used for music, except a CD-ROM is used in conjunction with a *computer* for storing and retrieving large amounts of information, as well as pictures and sounds. A CD-ROM can store both the information and the software to use it, all on the same disc. Short for "Compact Disc-Read Only Memory," but if you think about that definition too long, it'll make it more complicated than it really is. There is still confusion about whether CD-ROM means technically only CD-ROM, and not things like CD-I and CDTV, or whether CD-ROM refers to the family of technologies and includes all of them. In this book, it is usually used to mean the "family" concept.

**CD-ROM drive:** Also called a CD-ROM player—the piece of equipment that is hooked up to the computer, that you put the CD-ROM disc into.

**CD-ROM XA:** An enhanced version of CD-ROM, giving it the ability to store more sound and make the pictures and sounds work better together. Short for "CD-ROM Extended Architecture."

**CDTV:** A consumer version of CD-ROM, designed to be connected to a television set—made popular by Commodore. Short for "Commodore Dynamic Total Vision," but don't you think it should be short for "CD on a TV?"

**compression:** Using mathematical techniques to shrink the amount of space that it takes to store information. That way you can store more in less space.

**content:** What's inside or on a CD-ROM—just like the contents of any package. It's the text, data, pictures, sounds, on a CD-ROM.

**database:** An overused word meaning just about anything these days. Essentially it's a large amount of information that is organized on a computer.

**Data Discman:** Just like a Discman used for music, except it has a little keyboard and pop-up screen, and plays smaller versions of CD-ROM discs.

**delivery:** The way the information is sent, packaged, or transmitted to the end-user. Examples of ways to deliver information are CD-ROM, online, floppy disk, book.

**Digipack:** A new cardboard container to package CDs. Bonnie Raitt and Sting made attractive use of this packaging with their CDs. This is the brand name for the packaging made by AGI, but there is lots of work going on in the area of alternative packaging.

**digital:** Something that's stored in a form that the computer can understand (as opposed to stored on paper or cassette tape that the computer can't read).

**digitize:** The process of putting something in a form that the computer can understand.

**disc:** This term, spelled with a "c", usually refers to shiny silver discs you can hold in your hand and that can be used with a computer, like a compact disc or laser disc.

**disk:** This term, spelled with a "k", usually refers to the traditional way of storing information on computer, like a on floppy disk or hard disk drive.

**DVI:** An enhanced version of CD-ROM, giving it better abilities to store and view moving images and sound, like a computerized videotape—an acronym for Digital Video Interactive.

**end-user:** The person who actually uses the CD-ROM, computer, or whatever the product is.

**fixed-field:** A database that is highly organized. Fixed-field software can sort, rank, average, and work with this type of information.

**Full-motion video**: Usually refers to video that can play at about 30 frames per second on a computer, which is a rate considered acceptable in the video world. Full-screen, full-motion video will play at that speed on the entire screen, as opposed to a small window.

**full text:** Information that is structured like a book, with chapters and headings, and was probably originally meant to be read from front to back. Full-text software means software that can find any word in this loosely structured information.

**gigabyte:** A heckuva lot of information—equal to 1,000 megabytes. In the CD-ROM world, a gigabyte is a little more than a single CD-ROM disc can hold.

**hardcopy:** A fancy word for something that's stored on paper instead of a computer.

**heading**: Topic, subject, or category. "Main Heading" is quite often a main topic, and specifically the words used to describe that topic (Airplanes, Cars, etc,). A sub-heading is usually the next level(s) down from the main heading, like a sub-topic or sub-category.

**High Sierra Group:** A bunch of people who got together to make sure CD-ROM discs could play in all manufacturers' CD-ROM drives.

**indexing:** The computer builds a bunch of tables, similar to an index in the back of a book, so that it can later look things up more quickly. Indexing is the word used to describe that process of building the indexes. Indexing is also used in the information industry to describe the process a person goes through to siphon information from an article, resulting in a series of words used to describe and find the article, called an index.

**interactive multimedia:** Think of it as a videotape or movie that you can stop at any time and ask it questions, or respond to questions it asks. It's the current term to describe CD-ROMs that have lots of pictures and sound.

**ISO 9660:** After the High Sierra Group published its paper describing how to play CD-ROM discs, the International Standards Organization (ISO) formalized it, and the document, or standard, was called ISO 9660.

**jewel box:** A very strange word to describe the little plastic containers that CDs or CD-ROMs are packaged in. They usually crack, are impossible to open if you have them upside down, and we all hope they come up with something better. They're working on it—*see* **Digipack.**

**keyword:** The word that is being looked for on a computer. Keyword searching is typing in a keyword and telling the computer to find it.

**kilobyte:** Not a lot of information, and not too little, but somewhere in between. It's equivalent to 1,000 bytes and since a byte is an alphabetic character, it's 1,000 characters.

**mastering:** Making a single copy of something, exactly how you want it, before you mass produce it. Mastering in CD-ROM usually refers to the process that happens at the factory before they make thousands of discs.

**mastering facility:** A factory where CD-ROMs are mass-produced.

**MB:** Megabyte

**megabucks:** What everyone is hoping to make out of CD-ROM.

**megabyte:** The most socially acceptable member of the byte family, and equivalent to about how much data one floppy disk can store. A CD-ROM disc holds a little over 600 megabytes.

**memory:** What the computer either stores and/or how much processing power it has. It's a single word which can mean—using a car as an analogy—either horsepower (generally referred to as RAM) or amount of gas in a tank (generally referred to as a hard disk, or in the case of CD-ROM, it's the ROM).

**Microsoft extensions:** A piece of software for using a CD-ROM disc on an IBM-compatible computer. The formal name is MS-DOS CD-ROM Extensions.

**Microsoft show:** A once-a-year trade show originally sponsored by Microsoft. It has traditionally been the main conference of the CD-ROM industry, and has changed its name to Intermedia. A prediction: it will change its name again, but will continue to be known in the industry as the "Microsoft show."

**MMCD:** A technology from Sony that is somewhere between a Data Discman and a portable computer.

**MPC:** A way to make it easier to sell and buy CD-ROMs and computers that are used for multimedia. It's like a secret handshake between the manufacturers and the buyers of computers and CD-ROMs signaling a passion for multimedia.

**multimedia:** Pictures, sound, data, animation, all on a computer.

**numeric:** Something that is made up of numbers. 1234567 is numeric, but ABCDEFG is not.

**one-off:** A disc, as well as the machine that makes the disc, which is made one time with a writable CD-ROM machine. Instead of having a final disc made at the factory, which can be expensive and time-consuming, you can make a "one-off" disc with a "one-off" machine in the privacy of your own office. The machines cost under $10,000, a single blank one-off disc is just over $25 a piece, and it takes a half-hour to an hour to make the disc.

**online:** In the information industry, it means information that is used over a computer network connected to a distant computer.

**optical disc:** A family of technologies or discs that use a lasers to read the information from a disc using a computer to control it. A CD-ROM is one of the discs in the optical disc family.

**Photo CD:** Kodak's version of CD-ROM, which adds the ability to put your own pictures on a CD and view it through on a television screen.

**platform:** A family of computers. There's the DOS platform, the Macintosh platform, the UNIX platform, and so on.

**premastering:** A word, and not a pretty one, meaning the series of steps that happen before a CD is made at the factory, but after the initial development steps are done.

**query:** Asking the computer a question by typing something on the keyboard.

**Red Book:** A document that is red. Red Book is the official term used for the official document that describes how to make a CD music disc according to standard specifications.

**retrieval software:** Software used to find and display things on a computer.

**searching:** Finding things on a computer.

**standards:** Formal rules that industry manufacturers, such as CD-ROM drive manufacturers and factories that produce CD-ROMs, follow so everything works the way it should.

**text:** Words, letters, sentences, and anything else formed by using the 26 letters of the alphabet and numbers

**title:** In CD-ROM lingo, a title usually means a finished, packaged CD-ROM disc—similar to the way "book title" is used in the publishing business.

**transfer rate:** How fast the computer can transfer information from the CD-ROM disc to the computer—the faster the better.

**virtual reality:** Wearing goggles and gloves attached to a computer to simulate being in another world.

**VIS:** Tandy's version of CD-ROM. Short for "Video Information System."

**Yellow Book:** A document that describes how to make a CD-ROM.

# Acknowledgements

Many people were instrumental in getting this book off the ground.

The people at Pemberton Press Inc. and Online Inc. have been supportive of my ideas for many years, and this book would not have happened without their vision and support.

All the people mentioned in this book provide a vast landscape of ideas, thought, and personalities, without which CD-ROM would have stopped dead in its tracks years ago. They are all leaders in the field—I was fortunate enough to have been in the right places at the right times to see the events described in this book.

Thanks to Ned Worthington for valuable critical commentary.

Mary-Chapin Carpenter provided the background music which, if you listen very carefully, you can hear throughout the book.

I am especially grateful to Veronica Andrews, my wife, whose perceptive comments helped steer me in the right direction when the book was no more than a few pages and lots of ideas.

A special thanks goes to James, for waiting an extra couple weeks to make his entry into the world.

Christopher Andrews
March 1993

# —Books Currently Available Or Soon To Be— Published By Eight Bit Books

• ***The Education Of A CD-ROM Publisher*: *A Behind-The-Scenes Tale of Multimedia Intrigu*e** by Christopher Andrews. A fun and informative look at one of the most promising technologies of the nineties. Here, for the first time, get an insider's candid and humorous view of CD-ROM's rise from its origins in library reference to the heights of the entertainment world. Available now.

• ***CD-ROM Buyer's Guide & Handbook: The Definitive Reference For CD-ROM Users, The Third Edition Of CD-ROM Collection Builder's Toolkit, Revised and Expanded*** by Paul T. Nicholls. The definitive reference for CD-ROM users. Available now.

• ***Environment Online...The Greening Of Databases.*** The complete environmental series from *DATABASE* magazine, plus cited columns from *ONLINE* and *DATABASE*. Available now.

• ***Secrets Of The Super Searchers*** by Reva Bash. Top online searchers, in a series of interviews, share their secrets and demonstrate how they approach typical database search problems. Available Mid-1993.

• ***Online Search Strategies And Tips: The Best Of* ONLINE & DATABASE *1988-92*.** A newly compiled collection of the best articles we have published on planning, executing and outputting an online search. Available now.

• *Cumulative Index To* **ONLINE, DATABASE & CD-ROM** ***Professional: 1986-91.*** This cumulative index to the three leading professional journals of the database industry is expanded from the annual indexes to include book reviews and titles under author entries. The indexes for all three publications are merged into one handy reference. Available now.

• ***The Best Of CD-ROM Professional: Timeless Tips & Practical Advice.*** The most useful articles we have published from 1990-92...includes chapters on Publishing, Networking, Multimedia, Technology Trends, Practical User Tips and Top 20 Q & A columns. Available now.

• ***Computer Research On DIALOG—How To Make Your DIALOG Password Work Magic*** by Susanne Bjørner. How to use the world's largest databank to find crucial information for your career and personal life...information on companies, industries, people, places and events...where to buy products...plus thousands of facts and figures. Available Fall 1993.

• ***CD-ROM For Schools: The Definitive Handbook*** by Pam Berger and Susan Kinnell. A state-of-the-art overview of CD-ROM in schools, including an introduction to hardware, software and networking CD-ROM. This is a directory of CD-ROM titles described and evaluated with curriculum suggestions, ordering information, sample screens and more. Includes comparisons of major CD-ROM periodical indexes, encyclopedias and single titles; media center management, instruction, curriculum integration and funding issues; and a selective, current, annotated bibliography of articles and books. Available Fall 1993.

**Christopher Andrews** is president of UniDisc, Inc., a company he founded in 1989 that has produced such CD-ROMs as Guinness Disc of Records, the Grammy Awards CD-ROM, and The CD-ROM Directory *ON DISC*, as well as the ATP Tour Multimedia Tennis Scrapbook and the Clinton Economic Conference CD-ROM due to be released in 1993. Prior to starting UniDisc, Mr. Andrews held CD-ROM management positions at Meridian Data, Hewlett-Packard, and NewsBank, spearheading pioneering CD-ROM efforts at each company.

Mr. Andrews has developed tools that are used for CD-ROM publishing, including software and publishing systems. Prior to CD-ROM, Mr. Andrews worked for Information Access Company and I.P. Sharp, in the online information field.

Mr. Andrews has written over a dozen articles on a wide variety of topics for publications such as *CD-ROM Professional*, *Information Today*, and *CD-ROM EndUser*, as well as the *NARAS Journal*, a publication of the National Academy of Recording Arts and Sciences, and *Uniform Monthly*, the publication of the UNIX community. He is Contributing Editor to *The CD-ROM Directory*, and he has authored the industry commentary on a CD-ROM market research publication *Facts and Figures*. Mr. Andrews has taught numerous classes on CD-ROM publishing, including "How to Publish Your own CD-ROM," and "From Print to CD-ROM: Making Books Into Discs." He has spoken at major industry conferences around the world, including the Society for Scholarly Publishing, the ONLINE/CD-ROM Conference, and the International Conference on CD-ROM, on topics ranging from technical publishing to entertainment.

Mr. Andrews lives in Soquel, California with his wife, Veronica and son, James.